SHANE MACGOWAN
LAST OF THE CELTIC SOUL REBELS

Ian O'Doherty

BLACKWATER PRESS

Editor
Antoinette Higgins

Design & Layout
Paula Byrne

ISBN
0 86121543 5

© – Ian O'Doherty 1994

Produced in Ireland by
Blackwater Press
c/o Folens Publishers
8 Broomhill Business Park,
Tallaght, Dublin 24.

CONTENTS

ACKNOWLEDGEMENTS

The author would like to thank the following people for their cooperation and help.

John O'Connor of Blackwater Press, for taking the risk and going for a music book.

Antoinette Higgins, my editor for showing patience and understanding above and beyond the call of duty.

Michael O'Sullivan, for arranging the introduction to Blackwater Press, for tormenting and encouraging me as the situation demanded, but, most importantly, for always being ready to listen and give advice.

Gerry Scanlon for taking the time to organise the things I could not, for being irrepressively positive when things looked bleak.

Damien Corless for reading through the original manuscript and making some crucial suggestions and corrections.

Alan Corr for not laughing when I first mentioned the idea and for keeping the beer and advice flowing during the year.

Ronnie Drew, Christy Moore, Mary Coughlan, Dave Fanning, Madeline Seiler, and so many other people (some of whom could not be named) who gave up their time to talk.

Karl and Chiara for being there (shucks).

John Bergin of Work Stations Ltd., for kindly providing me with a system that even I could use.

Pat Doyle for his time and creativity.

Terry Thorpe of *The Irish Times* and Gavin McClelland of *The Sunday World*, for getting me out of jam when others had let me down. Thanks.

Michael Beirne of *The Dublin Event Guide* for photographs supplied.

Mick Quinn and Cathal Dawson of Hot Press, and John Cooney of the RTE Guide for photographs.

Lastly, and most importantly, to Donal and Phyl O'Doherty, for more than I have space here to mention. Thanks.

INTRODUCTION

The Pogues first came to my attention in 1985 when I stumbled across them playing a gig in Mayo. The energy and vitality of that show, coupled with the manic intensity of the audience stayed with me for a long time. Their performance at Self Aid convinced me that the drunken outfit with the crazed singer I had seen in the Beaten Path the previous year had the potential to become one of the great bands of our time. Certainly Shane has done more than enough to book his place in the list of the best songwriters Ireland has ever produced.

All through the 1980s, when bands like The Smiths and REM were providing the soundtrack to my adolescence, MacGowan would spring up from somewhere and remind me of just what an awesome talent he is.

In many ways I liked The Pogues despite myself. Their uninhibited use of traditional instruments did not fit in with my white boy guitar rock record collection, be it The Velvet Underground or The Wedding Present, or the other two acts mentioned above but I was just about old enough to have a vague memory of punk, and if ever there was an embodiment of that spirit in the 1980s, it was Shane MacGowan.

The *Last of the Celtic Soul Rebels* is an unauthorised biography, but while I have no intention of writing a press release for Shane I am writing from a fan's perspective. The one thing I learned while researching this book is that while the stories of his excess will eventually fade into insignificance, his music will continue to be inspirational, enjoyable and downright beautiful for a long time yet.

Ian O'Doherty, Dublin 1994.

1
SELF AID

The Christmas of 1984 is seen by many as the time when rock music came of age. For years this hybrid genre had caused panic and consternation among the more conservative elements of the western world. But the release that year of the ground breaking charity single *Feed The World* changed the perception of rock music and its place in society irrevocably.

Jarred by the harrowing news images of an Ethiopia wracked by famine and a crippling civil war, the world was stunned into mute tears which reflected what appeared to be the death of a nation. But apart from the obligatory donation to one charitable organisation or another it seemed as if the Ethiopian crisis was destined to become just another entry into the filthy catalogue of disasters which the West deplored but did little about, and when the facts were examined, was in no small way responsible for.

For Bob Geldof, however, the situation demanded something more than the standard liberal hand-wringing, and the slightly jaded rock star responded in the only way he knew how.

Written in collaboration with Midge Ure, the duo came up with *Feed The World*, a well meaning but mediocre song that was going to require more than their rapidly diminishing reputations to get anything more than merely cursory publicity and air play.

Aware of this and the fact that were he to release the song under his own steam he would only be accused of trying to inject some much needed life into his own flagging career, he recruited the top names in the music business of the time. The resulting effort went on to take up residence at the top of the charts and become the biggest selling single of all time.

The resounding success of the record and the unprecedented publicity given to both the song (and more importantly its subject matter) only served to increase Geldof's appetite for his newly found role of Messiah for the masses. In a typically grandiose gesture he decided to gather all the members of his first project together and stage an open air concert.

The resulting event, 'Live Aid', still stands as the biggest logistical undertaking in the history of show business and with all the artists and business concerns involved giving their services for free the days of rock being debated in the Commons and being seen as a real threat to the social structure were over; temporarily at least.

This unusual marriage of rock and charity became chic and it didn't take long for other such events to be announced for other worthy and not so worthy causes. Farmers in America were to be saved by the imaginatively titled 'Farm Aid'. While this event and others were not as successful as their progenitor it seemed in the mid to late 'eighties that one could not have a breakdown in one's car without being descended upon by hordes of well meaning musicians writing songs and making heart felt pleas on television for your rescue.

Opportunists and charity workers everywhere became aware of this unusual phenomenon and it did not take long for plans for such a concert to be hatched in Ireland.

The event was to be called 'Self Aid' and it was to focus on the crippling Irish unemployment problem of the day which was exacerbated by a weak Government and an increasingly weary entrepreneurial class.

'Self Aid' was unusual for many reasons. It was the first of these events to come under sustained fire from numerous critics who felt that it was not the place of rock musicians to be absolving the Government of their responsibility. Many of these critics pointed out that, realising they couldn't save the world, some of the acts involved were now more concerned with trying to save their careers. While the furore continued as to whether those critics were making a valid point or merely being spoilsports, many people forgot what was perhaps the most relevant argument against such an event – Ireland did not have the talent in sufficient depth to hold a twelve hour non-stop musical extravaganza. While the international success of the likes of U2, Van Morrison, and Paul Brady was something of which a small nation could be proud, the vast majority of the acts on the bill would ordinarily have had a problem selling out at one of Dublin's local night spots let alone in an open air arena as large as the RDS.

The success of U2 had spawned a legion of bands such as Cactus World News and Big Self. Practitioners of big music with *ersatz* soul and precious little heart who felt that honest endeavour, rousing choruses, and charismatic front men would catapult them to international recognition. They were wrong but logical arguments and calls for a semblance of common-sense to be introduced were dismissed as the tired bleatings of professional cynics. After all, the show must go on.

The event kicked off at midday on 17 May 1986 with that perennial nice guy Brush Shiels.

Shiels belonged to the first generation of Irish rockers and had played with both Phil Lynott and Gary Moore. While he was spared their capacity for self destruction he had none of their talent and has spent the last fifteen years playing a professional 'cheeky chappie' Dubliner with a sparkle in his eye, a funny but harmless story on the ready and a nice sing-along number on his ever present guitar.

It was particularly fitting that Shiels opened the event, which was, at the end of the day, an exercise in homespun optimism, fuelled with a kind of blind faith and an 'Is everybody having a good time?' tone which suited Shiels down to the ground. He was predictably bad but no worse than usual.

The general standard of mediocrity continued for five hours. The younger bands such as Blue In Heaven had hoped to make their mark on a large stage and in front of a bigger audience than they were ever to play in front of again but they suffered from the lack of interest of the crowd, most of whom had only arrived early to guarantee themselves good seats for the appearance of 'real acts' such as Christy Moore, Van Morrison and, who knows, there might have been a few there who wanted to see U2 also.

Twenty-past five in the afternoon saw the end of Those Nervous Animals. One of the more interesting and intelligent of the 'new breed' of Irish bands, they too had suffered from the apathy of the audience. It must have been disheartening for the young pretenders to see Ronnie Drew of The Dubliners achieve a better reaction from the crowd merely by walking on-stage than they had achieved by playing.

Dressed in black and looking better than he had for years, Drew looked happy to be there and it was with genuine pleasure that he introduced the next band.

That band were, of course, The Pogues. Sauntering on stage with the arrogance and unconscious swagger only held by born pop stars, Shane MacGowan and his cohorts raged through a twenty minute set that held all the urgency and vitality of the long forgotten punk era. With a cigarette in one hand and a bottle of Harp in the other, MacGowan launched into a blistering version of the *Sick Bed Of Cuchulainn*, followed by *Sally MacLennane* and a memorable version of *Dirty Old Town*.

Here was a man who was not interested in saving the unemployed, the rain forest or even his teeth. MacGowan, quite simply, kicked ass.

The excitement which greeted their set was an explosion of spontaneous appreciation for all that is good about music. Here was a man who looked as if he could be singing to his friends yet had twenty thousand people in the palm of his hand. Here were a band that looked as if they would be more comfortable busking in

Grafton Street and yet they were far more musically adept than many of their peers. Amidst the embarrassing display of false emotion from the other bands who begged to be liked or even tolerated, here was an outfit that looked as if they didn't really care and that is what really set them apart.

They played tin whistles! They played the mandolin! They broke all the stereotypes of the time as to what an Irish rock band should be and the crowd loved them for it. Here at last was a band other than U2 about which to get excited.

The arrival of the Pogues heralded many things, not least of which was the eventual acceptance by a rock audience of traditional instruments such as the tin whistle.

The energy of their performance was an obvious highlight and took many people, who were not fully aware of the band, by surprise. In an interview with American television Shane MacGowan was more interested in his rapport with the fans around him than in being interviewed. In a similar interview with RTE he was drunk and happy behaving in a way guaranteed to cause outrage amongst those who like their singers to be paragons of virtue, and equally guaranteed to endear him to those who like their singers to look as if they might have something to say. A star was born.

Given their new found role as the bad boys of Irish music it would have been easy for them to sneer at the sentiments and naiveté surrounding 'Self Aid' in the way that several British musicians had done after 'Live Aid', but during an interview with Dave Fanning a few months later they were the epitome of grace.

Asked by Fanning what they thought of the event Shane said, 'It was one of the best days I've ever had, me personally'. Tin whistle player Spider Stacy was equally effusive, 'It was a real thrill, being introduced by Ronnie Drew. And the way that everybody in the crowd ...reacted... because there were these people up there on the stage who were completely unfashionable and what they were playing was completely unfashionable yet nobody really gave a toss and everybody was just really up for it. It was just really good to see.' Eschewing glib answers and lazy dismissal here we saw the most controversial of the bands who played, the ones most expected to be snide about the well intentioned but ultimately fruitless event, being full of grace and apparently genuinely pleased to have been involved.

Of course it is also true that they benefited from the event more than anyone else involved so The Pogues had every reason to feel benevolent towards it. Granted, they had played two nights in the SFX a few months previous and this appearance had been in front of a predominantly rock audience, and it certainly had nothing like the impact of their RDS show.

While the crowd may indeed have been 'up for it', the enthusiasm and general acceptance of which Spider spoke was not entirely universal.

An interesting development was the vociferous, although not entirely unpredictable opposition to the Pogues from the established clique of traditional musicians.

While Ronnie Drew and his fellow Dubliners had always been accepted by the rock fraternity, this acceptance had as much to do with their hard drinking, hard living image as it had to do with their music. This is borne out by the fact that the likes of Moving Hearts, a band which had valiantly tried to mix traditional music with rock, while achieving a creditable level of success with the record buying public, saw their earlier promise fade to nought. In many ways this was to be expected. Moving Hearts had never really attempted to force their blend of light fusion on anybody, in fact they seemed at times to be almost apologetic and while Horselips had fused rock and trad brilliantly a decade earlier, to most of the kids gathered in the RDS they were just another name in the annals of Irish music history.

The Pogues, on the other hand, could never be accused of being boring or jaded and it was this unrepentant energy and contempt for what Shane described as 'a load of bollix and fucking elitist shit' that scared the self appointed guardians of 'pure' traditional music.

Rather than enjoy the energy of the music and take heart in the fact that the Pogues were introducing traditional music to a whole new generation of people who previously would have preferred to have their toe nails extracted than listen to this hitherto bastion of ultra-naff, the likes of Noel Hill, an accomplished concertina player, and other established members of the traditional folk scene chose to go on the offensive. MacGowan found himself the unwitting and unwilling figurehead in a cultural debate as to the legitimacy of the music the Pogues played and the validity, or otherwise, of their vision of Ireland.

Seldom had such venom been directed at a popular band by traditional musicians.

This tension came to a head on the BPFO (the BP *Fallon Orchestra*, a Radio 2 music and talk program) when Hill went on the offensive. It was a bizarre spectacle and one which many people felt to be unrepresentative as to how the media, and more importantly, the fans felt about the band.

Placed on the spot by Hill and journalist Joe Ambrose, the band understandably became defensive and retaliated, whereupon Ambrose called bass player Cait O'Riordan a pig. O'Riordan replied with the contempt such a remark deserved and responded by treating the audience to a string of porcine grunting.

O'Riordan had the good grace to apologise for her overreaction shortly afterwards.

Fallon still flinches when he thinks of the show. 'We just got a load of people into the studio and let them take it from there, we never thought that it would develop into this mad row with people becoming hysterical and insulting each other,' says Fallon. 'It was great.'

Indeed this was great radio, and people spoke about it for weeks, but the original point of the argument tended to become a little blurred.

In the traditional corner we had Noel Hill, Joe Ambrose *et al* claiming that the Pogues were trespassing on music they felt to be precious and that the Pogues were treating this 'holy ground' with contempt.

On the face of it, this argument would appear to have a certain basic and rather crude kind of validity. With the Irish language fighting a losing battle against obsolescence and other aspects of Irish culture becoming rapidly redundant in the face of an increasingly multi-cultural and more pluralist Ireland, many felt that the popularity of The Pogues would only help to further dilute another crucial aspect of national identity; traditional and folk music.

But they were missing the point entirely. Trad and folk music had become increasingly insular and with internecine struggles between practitioners of the art becoming more and more public, the whole genre was in danger of being seen as the musical wing of de Valera's mythical Ireland which would, sooner or later, disappear up its own backside and become completely irrelevant.

What The Pogues were doing was what musicians had done since the first man started to bang on a log. They were incorporating various, apparently irreconcilable, influences and fusing them together to create something new, a product that doffed its cap to the old styles but was interested in something altogether fresh and exciting and young and vibrant. In another departure from the standard tradition of most folk music, they were placing a greater emphasis on the urban as opposed to the rural.

This was a vital ingredient to their success and one which has been largely ignored by commentators.

Most of the band had grown up in London and Shane brought to his writing the perspective of a city boy. While traditional Irish folk tunes had largely been written from the emigrants point of view Shane wrote from that of an immigrant.

This is best exemplified by songs such as *The Old Main Drag*: 'In the cold winter nights the old town it was chill / but there boys in the cafes who'd give you cheap pills / If you didn't have the money then you'd cajole or you'd beg / There was always lots of Tuinol on the old main drag / And now I am lying here, I've had too much booze / I've been shat on and spat on, raped and abused / I know that I am dying and I wish I could beg / For the money to take me back to old main drag'.

It was this fusion of folk music with punk and the bleary eyed cross pollination of the traditional themes and topics of Irish folk music coupled with the world weary neo-realism of someone like Tom Waites that so angered and, more pertinently, scared the hell out of their opponents. At last, here was a voice that actually had something real to say about what it was like to be young and Irish, and that was an achievement that Noel Hill, and these scared, blinkered moral custodians could never match.

2
THE EARLY YEARS

Shane MacGowan was born in Kent, England on the 25 December 1957. He spent the bulk of his childhood in Puckaun in Tipperary, from where his mother Therese hailed.

Growing up in a farmhouse with thirteen relatives, she was well versed in the traditional rural Irish pursuits of singing, dancing and story-telling. This environment bred into the young Therese a love for the arts and after learning an impressive body of tunes and trying them out at many a fleadh-ceoil in the area, she soon decided to spread her wings and move to Dublin where she sang and tried her hand at modelling.

While in Dublin she met Maurice MacGowan, an artistic and literate Dubliner who, as well as having a love for poetry, shared her interests in music, from the standard traditional fare to the more eclectic blues and jazz records of the day.

It was this open and cosmopolitan environment that first fuelled a voracious appetite for all forms of music that was to later become such a distinctive aspect of MacGowan's writing.

As he said himself, 'When I was really little I was brought up by the people in Tipperary who knew millions of songs. It was real gut level stuff, music that has been handed down from generation to generation'.

Returning to the open house atmosphere of his mother's home was heaven to the inquisitive young MacGowan and like so many other children before in rural houses up and down the land he would stay up late and watch as the neighbours would arrive in and show off a party piece that would captivate the young child.

'Listening to and singing Irish music was a part of life. I had an auntie who played the concertina, an uncle who played accordion, cousins who played banjo and tin whistle'.

When he was 7 years old his father got a job as an administration officer with C&A, the British clothing firm. Maurice, Therese, Shane, and younger sister Siobhan moved to central London and while the big city of London, with all the anonymity and harsh indifference that goes with such territory was a world away from the close knit Irish family and community network, he never felt too lonely. There is an Irish scene in London and you never forget the fact that you came from Ireland. There are a lot of Irish pubs there and you hear a lot of Irish music on the jukeboxes.

He also had an uncle who ran an Irish pub in Dagenham in London and he spent a lot of time there as well, listening to the strains of Irish music in the air and, no doubt, smelling porter for which he was to develop such a prodigious appetite in later years.

Although the family were pretty settled in London at that early stage, the young MacGowan spent his summer holidays back in his spiritual home of Tipperary and was as eager as ever to listen to the songs being sung and the tunes being played.

Even at an early age MacGowan showed signs of high intelligence and in 1971 he was accepted into Westminster public school on the basis of this putative talent. There are not too many working-class Irish kids who manage to gain entry into such a bastion of English imperialism. Rather than buckle down and 'try and make something of himself' he got expelled before the year was out when he was caught in possession of a variety of drugs, most notably hash and acid.

It was a pattern that was to be repeated throughout his life and even at that early age he had developed a taste for more than just beer.

The family were justifiably worried but he was a head strong youth and soon he was spending his time wandering around

Piccadilly taking in the sights and observing the human flotsam and jetsam that a city such as London throws with remorseless regularity.

Having already gone through phases of listening to Black Sabbath, Led Zeppelin and disco and soul he found what he was looking for when, while working in a pub in Charing Cross, he stumbled across the emerging London punk scene.

As he said to journalist Ann Scanlon in her book *The Pogues: The Lost Decade*, 'Seeing The Sex Pistols changed my life – it changed loads of people's lives. Here was a band that just got up there and made really horrible noise and didn't give a shit. They were all our age and had dyed hair and wore brothel creepers, and it was just a question of, "yeah fuck it. I hate everything". I thought they were brilliant, the best group I had ever seen'.

Like so many kids of that era The Sex Pistols and everything they stood for, or rather, everything they stood against was like nothing he had ever experienced before. The initial optimism of the music of the previous decade had been replaced by and large by the homogenised musicianship of ageing relics who had taken too many drugs and sacrificed their enthusiasm for technical excellence. The Pistols were, quite literally, the antithesis to all of this. The Pistols (despite the musicality of Glenn Matlock) could not play, and this was worn as a badge of honour, a two-fingered gesture to the music of their elder brothers.

MacGowan was, by chance, there from pretty much the very start, and it was something he immersed himself in with a vigour and enthusiasm that would have surprised his teachers at Westminster.

'The whole scene was based on gigs at places like the ICA and going to night clubs that stayed open all night, taking speed and drinking Pernod – as opposed to going out to a disco with your mates, drinking beer, getting in fights and picking up some bird. The punk scene was completely asexual so you'd get both sexes hanging around together, not doing anything except staying out all night and dancing.'

This nihilism, the whole couldn't-give-a-fuck attitude expressed best by the scrotum tightening fury of *Anarchy In The UK* and its refrain of 'we don't care' was a welcome change from the plodding seriousness of what was going on around them at the time. At last, thought the previously aimless MacGowan, there was something he really could get his teeth into.

Bizarrely, what really made his name around London at the time, was the fact that somebody else got their teeth into him. Literally.

In the cold winter of 1976 it looked as if punk was going to explode out of the clubs and haunts and go over ground, the excitement of being a part of the whole scene was at its peak. While Bill Grundy had not yet been verbally abused by the Pistols, the previously sluggish main stream media was beginning to whip itself up into its periodic righteous frenzy and moral crusade against whatever tide of evil was about to sweep the nation's youth.

Shane and some of his mates were in the ICA looking at The Clash, 'and me and this girl were having a laugh, which involved biting each other's arms 'till they were completely covered in blood and then smashing a few bottles and cutting each other up a bit. Anyway, in the end she went a bit over the top and bottled me in the side of the head. Gallons of blood came out and someone took a photograph. I never got it (ear) bitten off – although we had bitten each other to bits – it was just a heavy cut'.

With typical understatement Shane, now going under the moniker of Shane O'Hooligan, had become a minor punk icon, he had shown the aspired to, but seldom achieved, contempt for the flesh and, 'People used to stop me in the street and say, "You're the guy who had his ear bitten off, you are great man".' Of course, his ear was still intact but a bit of publicity never hurt although, as he said himself, 'It's like the old story about the bloke who catches the fish, he says that it weighs this much and it's that big and within a couple of days it is a whale'.

By this stage Shane O'Hooligan was working in the famous Soho record shop, Rocks Off, and he had decided, in typical punk fashion, to get up and give it a go himself.

In typical Shane fashion the band had a controversial name, The Nipple Erectors, and even then Shane's ear for a tune shone through and their first release, *King Of The Bop/Nervous Wreck* became a minor punk classic. Unlike a lot of the bands that sprang up around that time they didn't immediately disappear without a trace, and after changing their name to the rather less confrontational The Nips, went on to release three more singles, *All The Time In The World, Gabrielle*, which is widely regarded as the best of the bunch, and *Happy Song/Nobody To Love*, which was produced by Paul Weller, a man who Shane had respected enough to issue a fanzine, *Bondage* in honour of The Jam.

A live album also swam to the surface in the shape of *Only The End Of The Beginning*.

Like so many bands of the time, the membership was fluid to say the least, and in the few years of their existence, the only permanent fixtures were Shane and his pal Shanne Bradley. Interestingly enough, James Fearnley, who was later to play with The Pogues was playing with them when The Nips broke up in the winter of 1980.

Punk was a vital time for the nascent song writer, for while he had always been enamoured with the story telling and lilting musicality of the music of his parents, the whole explosion of the mid to late seventies infused him with a sense of energy and chaos that was to become such an essential ingredient in The Pogue's Irish stew.

During this time the community and sense of solidarity of the whole movement had introduced MacGowan to an array of like minded people. The Nips might have bitten the dust but there was little chance of him retreating from the music scene. While he had to go through a six-week drying out period following the break up of his first band he was as determined to stay in music as he was to continue drinking. At a Ramones gig a few years earlier he had met Spider Stacy, a man with no apparent musical ability but an abundance of attitude and an infectious sense of enthusiasm that endeared him to those he met.

Stacy was involved with an outfit called The Chainsaws, later to be known as The Milwall Chainsaws, where his duties consisted of screaming into the microphone and banging his head with a beer tray in approximate time to the music. At the time MacGowan was principally a guitarist and according to Stacy, 'For the kind of stuff we were doing Shane was perfect. He knew exactly what was required. Technically he's not a good guitarist but in terms of feel and energy he's brilliant'.

MacGowan had also rehearsed with bass player Jem Finer following the break up of The Nips. Finer had fluked his way into a combo that was knocking around at the time called The Petals, and he had developed a taste for the fun that being in a band at that time guaranteed.

For the next year and a half MacGowan, Stacy and Finer played around in a number of bands, sometimes playing together, sometimes separately and while they were rehearsing together the seeds of what was to become Pogue Mahone were sown.

In the summer of 1982, Fearnley was approached by MacGowan with a view to getting involved in music and after seeing the band play in The Pindar club, he decided that he was in.

Shortly afterwards, a young girl who had befriended Shane, Cait O'Riordan, came along and the loose band arrangement that had existed up until then began to solidify. Pogue Mahone, previously just a name to be used when the motley crew were playing one of their chaotic gigs, began to develop into a real band about which to get excited.

Up to this stage the band had concentrated on doing razzed up versions of old favourites such as *The Auld Triangle* by Brendan Behan and numerous old stamp-along numbers made popular by The Dubliners. Already however, Shane had written early versions of *Streams Of Whiskey* and *Dark Streets Of London*, with Shane playing guitar and singing, Spider banging his head off whatever percussive instrument was near, preferably a beer tray, while Finer and Fearnley tried to keep some manner of structure going but invariably went along with the flow and just enjoyed themselves.

But there was more to them than was immediately apparent, as Scanlon says, 'The Pindar crowd had already sensed that this was the beginning of something special when the band played *Waltzing Matilda* – a version so moving that even the obnoxious Stacy was reduced to tears. "The refrain at the end hit an emotional nerve", he said, "and I just started crying. It was really embarrassing"'.

Embarrassing for Stacy it might well have been but it shows that even at this stage MacGowan was probably more effective when singing something that sounded as if it was coming from his heart. It was an early indication that while MacGowan might never be considered one of the greatest singers to grace music in recent years, as a communicator he had few peers even then.

3
POGUE MAHONE

Cait made her debut for the band supporting the new wave troopers King Kurt in the 101 Club in Clapham. At the time King Kurt were probably best known for the novel stage accoutrements which they brought with their show. While Ozzy Osbourne was famous for biting the heads of live bats and assorted unsavoury but undoubtedly newsworthy exploits, King Kurt could not afford to bring fresh livestock with them to every gig so they made do with covering the stage with the internal organs of numerous small animals. While one can imagine Osbourne going into a pet shop in disguise and pretending to be an animal lover, it was more King Kurt's style to hang around outside the local butchers and take the stuff that would ordinarily be thrown out.

Said Jem Finer after the gig, 'It was absolutely disgusting. The stage was covered in goo so that every step you took you stuck to the floor. I trod on this thing that squelched and flew out from under my foot. I looked down and it was a rabbit's kidney, and there was a rabbit's head just lying there. Disgusting'.

Disgusting it may have been but a gig is a gig and Cait played on (wo)manfully ignoring the chaos and rabbitoir around her and the sound of Spider killing another beer tray with his head.

They soon decided that it was time to actually record some demos as opposed to listening to the rough recordings that they made through the PA when they were playing.

Using an old four track portable studio, they went to a friends flat and laid down *Waltzing Matilda*, *Streams Of Whiskey* and *Poor Paddy*. Due to basic errors made while recording on a basic machine the end result was less than satisfactory.

Undeterred by that minor disappointment, they soldiered on, going nowhere fast. Playing every gig they could get to gain much-needed experience, it was obvious that something was going to have to give in the band. Drummer John Hasler was widely regarded by his band mates to be the worst drummer they had ever had the misfortune to see, let alone play with, while Spider's tendency to, quite literally, headbang his way through a gig was beginning to wear thin with his cohorts as well.

Shane had reassured his friend that his place in the band was safe but worried by the looks from the other members he decided to try something that would justify his position as something more than resident screamer and shouter. So he started the tin whistle.

'I found it easier than I thought I would', he was to say later. 'It's a good instrument to pick out a simple tune on, the fingering is very logical and straight-forward. I got this book which had diagrams of the finger movements for tunes like *Amazing Grace* and *Silent Night*'.

Stacy's new found interest in a bona fide instrument, however unlikely, was helped by the fact that he learned how to play *Silent Night* within the first day of trying to learn. Truly a musical genius!

While the problem with Spider seemed to be somewhat resolved, the problem of the drummer remained. By Christmas of that year John Hasler was issued the warning that either he tried that little bit harder or he would be sacked. Realising that no matter how hard he tried it was unlikely to make him any better he decided to leave before facing the ignominy of being sacked by a band with a guitarist who couldn't play very well, a singer who was always too drunk to sing properly, a girl bass player who could throw a better punch than most blokes, and a tin whistle player who could only play *Silent Night* and who preferred screaming and belching into the microphone while banging his head repeatedly with a beer tray. Bad move.

The new year looked as if it would be the last for Pogue Mahone, Shane's drinking had become worse than ever and the rest of the band were not far behind him in the 'From Beer To Eternity stakes'.

While working in Rocks Off, Shane had met Phil Chevron. Chevron had first come to his attention with the Radiators From Space, the best of the Dublin bands around at that time. As the man responsible for such songs as *Under Clery's Clock* he was a talent far greater than anyone else at that time, with the possible exception of a slightly younger Paul Cleary who was beginning to emerge with The Blades.

Following the break up of the Radiators, a disillusioned Chevron went to London to take a look at what he was going to do with himself. At the behest of Shane he went down to Dingwalls one night to have a look at Pogue Mahone and he was not impressed at what he saw, 'I thought they were dreadful', said Chevron afterwards. 'But there was the knowledge that if they could get it right and sort out the line-up then they would work out a treat'. Top of the line-up-shopping-list was a drummer.

And lo, a drummer was delivered unto them. Andrew Ranken was known by most of the band and after some persuading the twenty-nine year old drummer played his first gig with them in the Hope And Anchor in Islington at the start of March 1983.

The addition of Ranken was exactly what the band needed, a steady drummer with an interest in how the rest of the music was shaping up. What had started off as a critical year for the band, with a genuine doubt as to whether it was worth while carrying on took off with a whole slew of well received dates around the greater London area.

However, the one bane that seemed to beset the band with frightening regularity was drink and the problems it caused. Shane in particular was developing, or rather continuing, his ridiculous consumption but despite the inevitable botched gigs and slurred performances the band had garnered an impressive reputation. While they were too wild for any of the record company A&R men to take a gamble on investing any money in them, they impressed industry figures to the extent that they topped an end of year Music Week poll as 'the band most likely to succeed'.

Just over a year since their inception, Pogue Mahone were knocking on the door marked 'big time'.

What they really needed was someone who had genuine experience in the music business who would have the patience to put up with their antics and someone they could trust enough to advise him.

That person was Frank Murray. Hailing from Drimnagh on the south side of Dublin, Murray had worked his way up from being a music fan to roadie with local bands to eventually working as tour manager for the likes of Thin Lizzy and Elton John. Murray was interested in getting involved with a couple of bands around this time, in particular The Men They Couldn't Hang, an earnest, politically oriented cow punk band that were beginning to establish their reputation around the same time as Pogue Mahone.

Murray saw the band in Islington, and like Phil Chevron a few months before him, he saw through their obvious cracks and felt that there was a band of genuine potential hiding timidly behind the drunken facade they portrayed. Murray was into bands like The Dubliners and their unpretentious attitude towards folk music as well as their flexibility. As he said later, 'I wasn't sure what it was that hit me about The Pogues, but they just got better and better. They did *Dirty Old Town* and *Peggy Gordon* and then Cait came out for the encore and sang *Don't It Make My Brown Eyes Blue*. Yet at the same time, the whole stage was so dishevelled that they were like a total mess: there were people bumping into each other all over the place. It was kind of slapstick, except it wasn't feigned and there was nothing pretentious, they were just having a great time'.

But just as Chevron had decided to give them a few months to find their feet, so did Frank Murray and they ended the year on a high but still looking after their own affairs.

1984 took off with a bang and in many ways it was to be the most important year of their career. In January they recorded their first single proper, *Dark Streets Of London* in the London's popular Elephant Studios. It was a studio they were to use extensively throughout their career and where Shane was later to record his first solo album, *The Snake*.

It was fitting that they chose to put *And The Band Played Waltzing Matilda* on the flip side, seeing as it was one of the earliest indications that there was more to the band than drunken high jinks.

The next month, on the back of their increasing live reputation, they were invited to record a session for the John Peel Show on Radio 1. Peel sessions were an invaluable help to many a band's career and there is hardly an outfit in the last fifteen years which has not used the session system to give themselves a leg up the career ladder.

Rather than re-record their recent single they went back to their first, aborted demo and did *Streams Of Whiskey*, *The Auld Triangle*, *Greenland Whale Fisheries* and *The Boys From The County Hell*. Unlike most other bands of the time, and indeed now, they treated the session slot with scant respect, and showed up drunk, cursing and generally obnoxious, the language on *The Boys From The County Hell* resulted in it being shelved and only the first three tracks were recorded.

Shortly after that session was done the band pressed two thousand white copies of their four track single. It caused an immediate buzz and all the energy and attitude of their live shows was at last down on vinyl.

Following a three-night support slot to The Clash in the Brixton Academy which was remarkably successful given that they were playing in front of a crowd not known for their tolerant attitude towards support acts, the band headed up to the Black Country for their first gig outside the metropolis. In the manner of all the best football clubs they brought a small army of travelling fans with them to ensure voluble support and, hopefully, to cover their costs. To everyone's surprise they did, and it was one of the few times the band were pleased with the state of their finances. 'The trip was astonishingly successful', Finer said to Ann Scanlon later, 'we filled the coach up with Pogue Mahone fans, and it all went off very well except that these people were completely mad. They all came on with at least twelve packs of beer, and it was obvious that something horrendous was going to happen'.

Something horrendous did indeed happen. On the ride back down to London the toilet in the coach broke down so they had to make regular stops to relieve the rather full bladders of the assembled throng. This would have been no more than a minor inconvenience in itself, but in addition the septic tanks of the coach had ruptured and when it came to extracting their gear from the bowels of the coach they discovered that everything had been soaked in urine. Thankfully, there is no record of the conversation that followed this particular discovery.

Their first TV appearance soon followed, a regional documentary on the sudden rise of country music among young bands. Presented by a pre Friday/Saturday Night Live Ben Elton, the band did not impress him saying, 'I think it will be a while before Pogue Mahone – Gaelic for Kiss My Arse by the way – will be seen on Top Of The Pops. Some of the other bands may stand a better chance of breaking through to a wider audience'. The other bands were The Shillelagh Sisters, The Boot Hill Foot Tappers and The Skiff Skats.

Their increased public profile inevitably led to queries about their name, and Ben Elton was not the only person to call attention to it. According to popular legend, there are a few different reasons why the name was eventually changed to The Pogues.

The first is that there was a native Irish speaker in the printing press where the *Dark Streets Of London* was pressed, and the fuss he made persuaded the band that the name would just cop too much flak in the future so they decided to drop it. The other is that a similarly inclined producer in Radio Scotland heard the name and freaked. Like so many Gaeilgeoir he didn't like the idea of his beloved language being besmirched by these foul mouthed hooligans blah, blah, etc.

The main reason, however, is that when Stan Brennan, long time friend of Shane and backer for the band went to the record companies to try and secure a distribution deal they were all put off by the name and the fact was that they would have trouble getting it played. Radio 1 had already decided to give *Dark Streets Of London* zero rotation, which they were quick to point out was not a ban, they just felt it was likely to cause offence to native Irish speakers and therefore they would not play it before 10 p.m. In effect they had consigned it to the John Peel show, which was influential but did not have a wide audience.

It was not the last time Shane & co. were to have trouble with the BBC, who had learned that banning records could be counter productive. The most obvious recent case of that occurred when Radio 1 disk jockey Mike Read became suitably irate after playing 'Relax' by Frankie Goes To Hollywood. That song had been falling down the charts when Read decided to object to its content. The publicity the band garnered from this objection promptly sent the song to Number 1 and secured their immediate career, and Reed's name, as the man who saved a group's career by trying to have them banned.

Stiff Records decided to take a risk where other companies would not and after getting the band to agree to change their name (there was no real row as none of the members had liked it very much anyway) they released *Dark Streets Of London* again.

4
RED ROSES FOR ME

Having decided to change their name to The Pogues and being picked up by Stiff, The Pogues could now consider themselves a 'real' band, but while they had come a long way from the barely controlled chaos of their earlier incarnations, they remained the same type of personalities.

Rather predictably, the glue which held them together was their shared love for drink and other stimulants.

While Stiff initially agreed to release just the one single, *Dark Streets Of London*, they kept, in typical record company fashion, the option for the first album, should The Pogues ever stop drinking long enough to record one. 'When we signed to Stiff, we had to pretend to stop drinking', said Shane. 'So in the photo sessions we had to hide our drinks. And in the pictures we look really miserable and uncomfortable because we are sitting on our beer cans'.

In the middle of June 1985 the band were playing in The Diorama in London. One of the many curious punters was Elvis Costello, who had been directed towards the band by the increasingly enthusiastic Phil Chevron. Struck by the energy of the band, and the sight of their uncommonly pretty bass player Costello went away with a head full of The Pogues and marked them down for future reference. So much so that he got in touch with them a few days later and invited them to join them on tour in Ireland a few months later.

Up until this time Cait had been playing relatively regularly with another North London outfit, Pride Of The Cross, playing mainly MOR favourites, she sang such numbers as *Peggy Lee's Fever* and *The Day Before You Came* by Abba (which was to be covered brilliantly by Blancmange around the same time).

Although she had recorded one single with Pride Of The Cross, *Tommy's Blue Valentine* (a tribute to the brilliant Tom Waites, whose path was to cross with The Pogues in the near future), she realised that sooner or later she was going to have to choose between one or other of the bands. Unlike the unfortunate John Hasler she chose The Pogues.

The Pogues then decided to go into the studio and record the debut album that they had been threatening to do since they signed for Stiff. Repairing back to The Elephant Studios in the sweltering August heat the began to work on *Red Roses For Me*, their stunning first long player.

Again, rather than buckling down and concentrating on finishing the album they continued playing and drinking, with the emphasis on the latter. The bouts of boozing often spilled over into bouts of fisticuffs, and in true rock and roll style, they were banned from playing again in the Wag Club in Wardour Street, after Cait got annoyed with Shane's behaviour and clocked him with her bass. The argument continued off stage and the other band members had to separate them physically backstage.

These scenes were to repeat themselves in true Jesus And Mary Chain fashion more than once and Jem Finer later said, 'Shane used to do really irritating things. We would learn a new song and then have an argument to get it into the set, and Shane would shake his head and say, "nah, nah, nah" and we would stand around for the next five minutes discussing what to play next'.

In later years, when Shane's drinking became not so much noticeable as completely unavoidable, people used to remark on his mistaking the introduction to a particular song as conclusive proof that he had finally lost it. In fact, this phenomenon was a fairly early and regular occurrence.

Playing The George Robey one night the band looked at their set list and started the opening strains of *And The Band Played*

Waltzing Matilda. All very well until Shane introduced the song as *Navigator* by Phil Gaston (later to appear as a brilliant cover version on *Rum, Sodomy And The Lash*).

Yet another full scale row ensued, 'which was on the verge of becoming physical when Cait butted in. Finer immediately turned from MacGowan to her: there was a pint glass at his foot and he took a well aimed kick. The glass shot into the air, flew across the air and finally shattered precariously close to O'Riordan's head' *(The Lost Decade)*.

After they finished recording *Red Roses For Me*, they began to prepare for their imminent tour of Ireland with Elvis Costello, which was to begin in The Ulster Hall in Belfast.

The tour was beset by problems, Elvis Costello's road crew were professionals, and thus less than sympathetic towards the lax attitudes of the young pretenders who had been invited on the road with them. Despite the problems brewing back stage the band took to such a large venue with alacrity, and though their promised £100 a gig appearance fee was all but swallowed up by the sound and lighting fees, they were enjoying the new experience thoroughly.

The tour continued to Galway when the band discovered that the road crew had, ever so accidentally, mixed-up The Pogues instruments with some oboes which had been left lying around The Ulster Hall by the BBC Orchestra. A hastily rearranged set was played on some borrowed instruments and the entourage headed to Dublin where they played the worst gig of the short tour. But never fear, ramshackle gigs were a familiar theme to The Pogues and after being picked up by Stiff, The Pogues could now consider themselves a 'real band' who were intent on coming back under their own steam and on their own terms.

They returned to London to prepare for the imminent release of *Red Roses For Me*.

Ten years later, the album is still invigorating, and while all the flaws that beset their live shows are present, they actually help to make the record the endearing little beauty it is.

In the pop climate of the day it is uncompromising and bravely unfashionable, given that they had to compete for airplay and attention with a whole rash of pretty bands, such as London's Spandau Ballet, and Duran Duran, who had escaped from the grim environs of Birmingham in a whirl of dodgy lyrics and equally dodgy clothes.

A rough and ready collection of their personal favourites which they had learned together while rehearsing (*The Auld Triangle* and *Greenland Whale Fisheries*) as well as Shane's own work (the opening *Transmetropolitan* and *Dark Streets Of London* their first single and still a classic to this day).

The aforementioned *Transmetropolitan* and the chaotic *Boys From The County Hell* led people to wonder openly about their political affiliations, and while such red herrings have dogged any band that attempts anything more adventurous than rhyming 'moon' with 'soon', Shane was not going to let himself be drawn into a debate that could cause the band more trouble than it would be worth, 'What we are saying is fuck everything, which is not the same as saying fuck so and so'.

And with more acceptable blanket condemnation of just about everything, the matter was closed, as far as the band were concerned, anyway.

5
A SORT OF HOMECOMING

The Pogues, supported by the Golden Horde, played at the Hammersmith Palais, on St Patrick's Day.

'The hippies used to describe things of such conceptual purity as 'happenings'. They'd go down to the park and tune on to whatever vibe the shaman was concocting, be it reciting poetry, beating the bongo's, or chanting in a foreign tongue. A sense of cosmic unity and wholeness would soon materialise. They would see God.

'The event of which we speak has connotations which are a little less, shall we say, spiritual.

'One anticipates a measure of bawdiness whose only precedent is a scene in the saloon the night before prohibition. Most of the audience will be blind drunk, or in the process of so becoming. They will be mentally and emotionally unstable. There may be public copulation. There may be fisticuffs. There is a sense of apprehension that one may walk away with this with one's personality altered for good. One may even die. But it is not to be missed. This concert may be signalled out by historians of the future. If the worst comes to the worst, they will speak of the St Patrick's Day massacre.'

So wrote Declan Lynch when he journeyed to England to review the band for *Hot Press* in March 1986 for their St Patrick's Day gig in the Hammersmith Palais. He recalls, 'The Hammersmith Palais was one of these very old, rather naff kind of places, where you would expect to see an old English gentleman in a shiny white coat conducting bingo sessions. I always remember that up the road the much bigger Hammersmith Odeon was playing host to Foster and Allen the same night. I remarked on this strange fact backstage with The Pogues and the good Jem Finer replied, "Well you can't knock them, can you?".

'"Why not?", was my answer, of course you can knock them, they are horrendous, an embarrassment, and they were all going, "ah, no, you can't really say that", I was amazed. I thought it was taking this whole London-Irish rock ecumenism thing a bit too far'.

The Pogues could afford to be generous in their opinion of other bands around this time, seeing as their star was very much in the ascendant. Their EP, *Poguetry In Motion* had just entered the Top Thirty in England, largely on the back of *A Rainy Night In Soho*, which had succeeded in getting extensive airplay in Ireland and Britain, while the first track from the EP, *London Girl* was also play listed by Radio 1 in England.

Between the combined crowds of The Pogues and Foster And Allen (or *Voerster And Outspan*, as Lynch dubbed them in reference to their appearance in South Africa) it seemed as if Harlseden had been transported to more a salubrious area of London and they did their best to drink the suburb dry.

One of the attractions of The Pogues to their fan base was the fact that the band seemed to have the same interests and pursuits as they did. Nowhere was this more obvious than in their shared love for drink.

Before and after the gig Shane held court back stage while swigging out of bottles of Sherry.

Eventually, the band dragged themselves onto the stage to the now customary rapturous applause.

Given the night that was in it, the fact that most of the crowd were off their heads with sheer enthusiasm and excitement as much as anything else, The Pogues could have played the spoons for all the critical faculties that were going to judge them.

Like so many of their gigs before, they were more interested in creating, as BP Fallon would say, 'a vibe'. The sense of community among the crowd, the sense of place, of sheer rightness at being there, was an experience similar to that of being at a football match watching your favourite team. Following The Pogues was like following Celtic, they might not always put in a vintage performance, but it is the effort that counts and anyway, the most important thing is to be able to say that you saw your heroes in the flesh. Just as it comes as no surprise to hear Celtic fans say with a smile on their faces that Celtic were shit the previous Saturday, it was no surprise to hear the occasional Pogues fan talk ruefully about how chaotic their last show had been. Pure analysis and logical criticism was for mere rock critics and Rangers fans.

While the band acknowledged this comparison, indeed they would have had to be blind to ignore it, it was not something they were particularly keen to foster and develop. As Phil Chevron said, 'I suppose we come across a bit like a football team, because we don't look like Duran Duran or wear Anthony Paul suits or John Paul Gaultier underpants, we look pretty much like the male members of the audience. Consequently we – and especially Shane – are regarded by other males as ordinary blokes that you could meet in the pub and have a drink with'.

However, while they were proud to feel that they held a kinship with their audience that was quite rare at the time, Chevron later mused that this almost tribal sense of identity did hold the potential to be counter productive, 'we can't get away from the fact that we will always see a load of Celtic scarves every time we play in the Barrowlands and elsewhere but I would hate to feel that a Rangers fan or anyone else felt that they could not come because they were not welcome, that is not what we are about'.

Lynch remembers his introduction to Shane after the gig with a sense of bemusement. 'I had met Shane about a year before at a press reception but because he was so wrecked that time, I wasn't so sure how well he recalled that particular night, and the fact that he seemed to be not too far away from a similar state that night in The Palais I decided to go about the rigmarole of formal introductions again. But, as it turned out, he did remember our first meeting and I think that because he is so pissed a lot of the time people just presume that he won't remember his own name, let alone that of someone else. But he does have a fairly good grip on things, even when he is plastered, and I think he gets a bit irritated having to interrupt people who have met him before and tell them that yes, he does remember the night they met, and yes, he does remember their name. I think at that stage he had just about given up doing that and was prepared to let people waffle away and not interrupt.

'It was around that time that the band, and particularly Spider Stacy had got into *Once Upon A Time In America*, the Sergio Leone gangster film, so it was all, "fuck you motherfucker, don't fuck with me or I will fuck with you", that type of rubbish, so any chance of getting some sort of valid, meaningful interview was unlikely to say the least.'

'Elvis Costello was spending a lot of time with the band around then, himself and Cait were a fairly established item by that stage, and it was amusing to see the irreverence of the band towards him. They spent most of the evening calling him "uncle" which I found pretty amusing.'

After the show, and when the back stage party had finally wound up, Shane and the band and the rest of the entourage retired to a 'kind of a warehouse' for some more partying when, 'Cait decided that she wanted to dance and that she wanted Elvis to dance with her. He didn't seem to be particularly into it but The Pogues took up the opportunity for some more slagging and a chorus of "come on uncle, you can do it" ensued. He wasn't too impressed, but what can you do?'

Shortly afterwards, following a ragged conversation with Shane 'about Catholicism and the influence of the Church in rural Ireland' Declan, tired from the conversation, the refreshments and the continuing presence of BP Fallon, decided to bed down for the night where he stayed with Stephen Cush, a long time friend, roadie of the band and one of the nicest people around, who was to die tragically in a car crash a couple of years later.

6

THE DUBLINERS CONNECTION

One of the most respected and admired figures in the Irish music scene, Ronnie Drew was one of the first to realise that labels cannot adequately describe music. As he puts it so succinctly himself, 'there are two types of music, good music and bad music, the rest is irrelevant'.

In many ways it was fitting that Drew and MacGowan should become friends and record together, given the fact that The Dubliner has spent nearly thirty years rocking the boat of cosy preconception and lazy ignorance in the traditional and folk music worlds.

They first met at the Vienna Folk Festival in 1986, 'and I remember it well, we hit it off from the start and I found him a very sensitive guy and we got on great with all the guys in the band. I was very gratified that he often said we had influenced him. I don't mean that in any big-headed way but it is nice to know that you are being appreciated, especially by younger people. And Shane, I suppose, was the spokesman for the younger people at the time in his particular area. We then got an idea later on that week when we asked him would he like to come in with us on a version of *The Irish Rover* which they were well into. It was a great thing for us as well because younger people could see that we weren't real 'fuddy duddies', just because I have a beard and I wear a suit. So we benefited a great deal from that as well'.

Whatever motivated Drew and the rest of The Dubliners to get involved with a band that were so obviously kicking up a storm, he was, and remains in awe of MacGowan's talent, 'he is a truly great songwriter, all you have to do is look at stuff like *Fairy Tale Of New*

York and *Rainy Night In Soho*, by any standard they are great songs'.

Interestingly enough, while Drew and the rest of The Dubliner's were aware of Shane and The Pogues before they met at the Folk Festival, he admits that he was 'quite sceptical, to be honest with you. But having spoken to the guy I realised that himself and the band were serious. Not so much that they took themselves too seriously, because they don't, but serious in the sense that they were very genuine and they cared a lot about what they were doing. And when he sings *Dirty Old Town* it is uncannily like Luke Kelly, and Shane himself admits to this influence which is a tremendous compliment to us'.

Madeline Seiler admits that when she saw Shane singing *Dirty Old Town* she was not too impressed, feeling that he was just doing an imitation of Kelly. While Drew can understand such scepticism, he doesn't agree. 'Shane is too original to do anything like that, his originality in writing and interpreting songs is one of the things that makes him so good'.

On the 6 March 1987 the world of Irish music gathered on the set of the Late Late Show to celebrate 25 years of The Dubliners. 'Stellar cast' is a cliché much over used to describe a bunch of musicians together in the same room but in this instance it is as an effective a cliché as any other. Taking their place along side The Dubliners, Christy Moore, The Fureys, Stockton's Wing, and U2, The Pogues fit in perfectly, straddling the divide between the old school of foot stompers and those who had fought the punk wars with consummate ease.

The Pogues joined their spiritual mentors on stage for a rousing version of *The Irish Rover*, a perfect synthesis forged between the two bands that, as Drew freely admits, 'opened us (The Dubliners) up to a whole new audience'.

The two bands had decided to get together and release the song and to nobody's great surprise, it took off like a porter fuelled rocket in the English and Irish charts. With the record approaching the top twenty they accepted an invitation to appear on Top Of The Pops, a welcome respite from what was appearing on the show at a time before the likes of The Stone Roses and Happy Mondays brought their own form of debauchery to the program.

Drew recalls that time with fondness. 'It had been twenty years since I had been on the show and I was looking forward to it, especially as it was with a gang that was as good crack as The Pogues'.

As Ann Scanlon wrote in her 1988 catalogue of The Pogue's rise, *The Lost Decade*, '"This place has changed a fair bit since I was here", remarked Ronnie Dew as he cast an eye around Studio Six. "When was that?" asked the floor manager. "1967", said Ronnie, to general laughter'.

The recording of the single had been a dream, taking only a few days and as neither Shane nor any of the others had screwed up, the general good vibes were repeated on the show. Despite the fears of numerous BBC producers who were afraid that these two mad Irish bands would come in and storm their precious little palace, and leave the place a smouldering wreck, both bands were the model of decorum, and that appearance has gone down in the annals of the show as one of those special moments that Top Of The Pops used to spring upon us with breath-taking regularity.

As Drew recalls, 'it was a great gig, it was good fun. At a time like that you tend to be watching other people to see how they are behaving but there was a real party atmosphere. At times like that you realise that it is not just about the money or the fame; times like that are special and few people ever get to experience anything like it'.

Like Christy Moore, Drew is somewhat nonplussed by the backlash that greeted Shane in 1986.

'I don't hold any particular medium of music as sacred, everything has to develop and has to change and evolve because it is a natural process, and a healthy and necessary one. As I said, I was cautious at first but as soon as I realised they were being honest I thought it was great.'

'There is a certain puritanical 'folk police' mentality going around which I don't subscribe to at all. The fact is that people are going to do things with music and if you don't it will stay static. The Uilleain pipes are a good example of this. They were played, the same way for so long and then you've got guys like Paddy Moloney and Davey Spillane doing new and adventurous things with them and they are now an international instrument. I don't believe that to be a 'pure' musician you have to be stuck in the same rut all the time.'

Surely there is something very ironic about the fact that certain practitioners of folk music, which was after all, the original people's music, are trying to dress it up as some sort of esoteric art, not suitable for the common lumpen proletariat? 'Exactly, like all other forms of music, once it stays the same it is basically fucked. Of course it is very important to respect the archival material and the roots of what we have today, and yeah, I think that the older stuff should be played more often on the radio and on television. But people like Shane who have progressed from that and made something valid should be congratulated and encouraged, and if I was him my attitude would be to tell them all to fuck off'.

One reason given by many people for such vociferous opposition for what Shane was trying to do was that, basically, they were jealous. Drew does not agree.

'I don't even think there was that much emotion in these people to be jealous, they just looked on what they were doing as some sort of job and they didn't like someone like Shane coming in and rocking their little boat, because they don't like to take chances the way Shane does, they just like to keep everything safe.

'A lot of that has to do with the way Shane looked and acted as well. People tend to place a lot of emphasis on image. Look at me for example, people tend to think that I am conformist because I wear a suit, but I have a very open mind, I just like to wear suits. And then when they saw Shane being drunk and generally acting in a way which they thought was unbecoming of how someone involved in any form of trad music should be behaving, they got all defensive and angry. But some of his critics wear suits in their minds if you know what I mean, they are very staid.'

'My theory is that if you are like Shane you can't always wait for the green man before you cross the road, you have to take risks in your music every now and then and he is quite prepared to do it. Sometimes it works and sometimes it doesn't and you just move onto the next idea but you have to keep trying, and that is what makes him so valuable. I hope to God he gets it together and makes a go of it again.'

Following Shane's controversial appearance at the '94 Fleadh, it appeared that the stories of his apparent rejuvenation had been greatly exaggerated. Drew had heard those stories as well, but he also played with Shane later that day.

'By the time he had come on with us he was great. I had heard all about him being off his head earlier in the day but we were not playing until the evening so obviously he had sobered up!

This thing about drinking is that it is an occupational hazard. It got a big hold on me as well. I just had to give it up, absolutely unquestionably. The thing is that anybody who likes drinking is playing with fire, some people get burned and some don't, that is the unfortunate fact of the matter. I got burned quite badly, and it is not something I would wish on anybody, and I hope that he can control it because it would be a terrible pity if we have to see such a great talent go to waste.'

Drew admits that he was lucky and that he got a lot of support, but there were a lot of people around Shane who were 'hangers on'. Even so, Drew does not feel that the proverbial 'slap around the head' would have been very effective. 'You can't really do that to someone, particularly someone like Shane, because what we are talking about is a medical condition here, not a punishable offence.

You really have to get someone who understands the problem because I know how hard it is to try and get off that particular trip and you need help and understanding more than anything else.

'The bottom line is that he really needs to want to do it for himself, but he still has time because he is only a young fellow, what age is he, 36? Jesus, I could be his father.'

'You see the public try to mould you into something that you are not, they want to think that someone like Shane can drink all the time then and give them lots of good drinking stories. But they don't want to see him drunk on stage, and they certainly do not want to see him forgetting the lyrics to their favourite song, so you find yourself stuck in a vicious circle that can kill you.'

A measure of how well-respected that MacGowan really is are the tones in which someone like Ronnie Drew speaks of him. MacGowan has written a song for him called *The Great Hunger*, one of the most brilliant famine songs ever written which Drew plans to release in 1995 to commemorate the 150 years since the start the Famine, and it is something that has excited the Grand Old Man of Irish Folk more than anything else in recent years.

'The song is absolutely brilliant', he says. 'It is very succinct and observant and it shows how important MacGowan feels his roots are. We share a common interest in things like this and I was very pleased that he gave me his imprimatur on the song, it is a great compliment to me, and any singer will know that is a great feeling to have a song written for you and an even better one when the writer thinks that you have done the song justice.

A lot of previous songs about the famine have been whingey, irritating affairs. But *The Great Hunger* deals with the anger of a child seeing his family being evicted and then shooting the men responsible. It is stark and chilling and one of the best things MacGowan has written in years, indeed it would be a shame if he were not to record it himself at some stage. The fury, anger and uncompromising tone of the lyrics are what really attracted Drew to the song.

'This shows the difference between MacGowan and a lot of other musicians of his generation. He knows a lot about the old ways in Ireland, which generally speaking is not why a lot of people get into a band; they are more into the whole idea of forming a group so they can become famous or they can get rich or get lots of girls or whatever and that should not be your sole reason for joining a band, although they can be enjoyable as well! But if they are your only reasons then it is just bullshit, you won't last, whereas Shane is into the whole thing because he loves it.'

The media trap is something of which both performers have become wary.

'The fucking journalists will have you jumping through hoops', he says with contempt. 'And Shane was perfect for them, he had everything they wanted, he was witty, he wrote great songs, he had a lot to say for himself and the whole drinking thing gave them a whole different angle to play with as well'.

While careful not to say anything that might be misconstrued, Drew also feels that he would be well advised to start looking after his own affairs himself. 'You have to be careful, especially when you are younger, about who you have controlling your affairs. I had that sort of hassle myself with previous managers, when they would tell me that I had to do something and I would just tell them to fuck off. If I want to do something I will do it, nobody will tell me what to do. You see, a lot of these guys (managers) think that you are working for them and you are not. It is the other way around and that line can get blurred at times. At the end of the day a manager is employed by you to do what you tell him to, and to look after the day to day operations that artists can't take care of all of the time. A lot of the time they can get very bossy and you start to think that what they say is Gospel. It isn't and that can be a very hard lesson to learn'.

It is undoubtedly a lesson that MacGowan has had to learn, although whether he has fully learned it has yet to be seen.

7

THE KELLY INFLUENCE

The band's performance at Self Aid was made even more notable by the fact that they had been introduced on stage by Ronnie Drew. Shane had long professed to be a fan of The Dubliners and in particular of Luke Kelly, the brilliant and mercurial singer, who indelibly stamped his mark on Irish music with his brilliant interpretations of such classics as Ewen MacColl's *Dirty Old Town*.

One person, however, who was worried by this adulation was Madeline Seiler. Seiler had arrived in Dublin in the 'seventies as a young student and while there she met and fell in love with Kelly.

She was understandably defensive about Kelly and had grown tired of hearing stories about the man while he was alive and now, with him eight years dead, she saw The Pogues performance at 'Self Aid' as a cheap, and somewhat shambolic shot by the band to be seen in the same tradition as her deceased lover.

Looking back on the gig she says, 'I was horrified at what I saw. I had heard a bit about the band but when I saw them in the RDS they just struck me as pretty untalented rip off merchants. They did not impress me in any way and their cover of *Dirty Old Town* was very weak, I felt.

It was only when I went to the Vienna folk festival in 1987 and I met The Pogues that I realised they were sincere in what they were trying to do.

'I met Shane that night and I got talking to him and it was very obvious that he was a genuine fan of what Luke had done and he was in no way trying to exploit his memory. I saw many things in Shane that were present in Luke, particularly the very sharp intelligence, and in a funny way, the same sense of loneliness when in a crowd. We got on very well that night and went on to become quite close friends.'

One of the most obvious comparisons to have been made about both men was their love for a drink and in many ways what appeared to be almost a death wish. A kind of bizarre drowning by alcohol.

This however, is something that Seiler rejects out of hand. 'For all the talk about Luke and his heavy drinking he was never as bad as people made him out to be. He loved a drink but then so did all of *The Dubliners* and Luke was as inclined to party as the rest of them but he never used it as a crutch and when he wasn't touring or involved with the band he never really cared whether he had a drink or not. Of course the band had developed such a reputation by that stage that he only had to be seen having a pint in a pub and all the stories would circulate about Luke going on the batter again.

'I remember numerous occasions when I was out and I would hear people talking about Luke in a conversation beside me and quite frequently I would hear people who I knew had absolutely no acquaintance with Luke at all saying how they had seen him blind drunk the night before, yet he would have been at home with me! This was quite distressing at times but you just try to ignore it, although I always found the pointless malice of it all rather inexplicable but it was something that you just had to learn to live with.'

But while Luke seemed to have some control over his drinking, that self control was not something exercised by Shane.

Says Seiler, 'the more I got to know Shane the more it became obvious that he really had quite a serious drink problem. When I met the band first they all had a reputation as being pretty serious party animals but that was almost to be expected given the circles they were moving in and the very lively personalities they all had.

But it soon became clear that Shane seemed to want it just that bit harder than any of the others. He hated touring and while he liked being in company he got tired of people very quickly if he did not find them stimulating. He used to get very edgy at times and there were so many people who wanted to talk to Shane MacGowan the performer or the pop star or the song writer or the drinker but there seemed to be very few people who wanted to talk to Shane MacGowan the person and that used to annoy him quite a lot'.

'We used to meet up in Dublin and just go for really long drives in the country and he felt he could relax then and he would be really sweet to people he would meet through me because they were all right and they did not make any kind of big deal about who he was and he found that very refreshing.

'He is undoubtedly one of the most intelligent people I have ever met and he is very sweet and sensitive but if he feels you are wasting his time or not being straight with him he has no problems with telling you to fuck off straight away.

'I remember though, when I would meet him in the mornings or the early afternoon and he would usually be quite tense until we went to a pub and you could actually see him relaxing as he had a few beers.'

She realised, however, in 1988 that things had gone beyond just a few drinks.

'Shane, like the rest of us, would like the occasional line of speed or maybe the occasional bit of coke but there was never any problem with that, it can actually be quite helpful when you are touring or being really busy and as long as you can keep it under control there is no real danger, although you have to be very aware that it can take control over you very easily if you are not careful. We went to the Cathedral Club one night and although Shane was looking for something, there did not seem to be any around, so it was just forgotten about. Later on in the night I was standing at the table while Shane went to the toilet and this really rough looking young lad came up to me. He was only about sixteen but he was very hard and a real Dublin hard 'chaw'. He was looking for Shane and we started to talk. It was obvious that Shane had spoken to him about getting some stuff and it didn't really bother me but then the young fellow said something, I can't actually remember, I think he used some term or something but it became clear to me that he was talking about Heroin. I just freaked. As I said, the occasional pick me up can be all right but smack absolutely disgusts me, I have never seen something to fuck you up as quickly and as badly as that shit, I absolutely despise it and everything surrounding it, it is a truly evil substance.

'I tried speaking to Shane when he came back from the loo but there was no talking to him, he is very good at blocking you out when he doesn't want to listen to what you are saying, he just dismissed it, saying, "ah, it's nothing to worry about" but you have to worry when heroin is involved.

'I kind of let it drop because I did not want to jeopardise our friendship by coming on too strongly but I was very worried and his behaviour did start to become affected by what he was doing.

'Matters came to a head one afternoon in Blooms Hotel when we were all having a few drinks before the band went back to England. The band left, and myself and Siobhan (his sister) stayed behind.

'I don't know why but at one stage in the evening I just started to cry, well not exactly cry, but tears just stared to roll down my face, I think I felt that I would never see him again he looked that bad.

'Siobhan asked me what the matter was and when I told her she was obviously very shocked, she had no idea he was into something that heavy.

'We ended up staying there for hours and I eventually persuaded Siobhan that she had to get him some help and that if he wasn't prepared to do so voluntarily she would have to admit him somewhere because I really felt that he would die if he kept going the way he was.

'Siobhan didn't really want to know at first because although she is a very strong person in her own way she was worried that Shane would see any positive action on her part as to be some kind of betrayal.

'This summed up the situation quite well for a lot of the people around Shane, they were concerned all right but for too long they were afraid of doing anything that might jeopardise their friendship or business relationship with him. But it is like anybody in a situation like that, you have to remember that the Heroin has taken them over and they are incapable of looking at things impartially, all they are concerned about is their next fix, nothing else really matters.'

Eventually, though, Siobhan realised that something had to be done and they agreed that they would try to persuade him to get some counselling, and if he was not agreeable, they would have to take drastic action.

'Siobhan committed him to the John Of God centre to be rehabilitated. He was, quite obviously, unimpressed with this and he definitely saw it as an act of betrayal by both Siobhan and myself.

'He was there for a few weeks and I knew this was the only way he was ever going to get better.'

8

IF I SHOULD FALL FROM GRACE

U p until the release of *If I Should Fall From The Grace Of God*, in 1988, most of the attention and praise showered on the band centred around Shane's singularly talented writing skills. While the energy and chaos that surrounded their gigs was thrilling in the extreme even the most devout Pogues fan would never claim that they were musically proficient. The recruitment of Steve Lillywhite as producer was seen by many people to be a strange choice. Lillywhite was better known as a producer of the likes of U2 and assorted other post-punk bands. It was not an obvious choice, but it was an inspired one.

Lillywhite brought out the often hidden musical interests of the band. Shane's North-London upbringing had brought him into contact with a diverse and multi-cultural melting pot of Greek, Jamaican and sundry other ethnic musical concerns and this was the final proof that behind a facade of drunken Irish jiggery pokery there was a musical brain at work that had no equal at that time.

If I Should Fall... displayed a more musically democratic theme than before. Jem Finer emerged as the instrumental master of the band, Terry Woods contributed the masterful *Streets Of Sorrow*, while Phil Chevron emerged from the wilderness with the angry, bitter and heart breaking *Thousands Are Sailing*, a stark lament for the generations of Irish people, past, present and future whose only hope was the emigrant trail.

One of the most interesting things about *If I Should Fall...* was that while the music had become more overtly eclectic Shane's lyrics had become more obviously Irish and inward looking. With the exception of the life affirming *Fiesta* and *Bottle Of Smoke* Shane unleashed his fears and demons in the most creative and seductive way imaginable, particularly on the song regarded by many to be his finest hour, *Lullaby Of London*.

Shane proved there was more to him than the drunk Irishman/happy Irishman through his ability here to enter his own heart of darkness and emerge, if not exactly unscathed, untainted by syrupy sentimentality and misty eyed self-pity.

Of course, *If I Should Fall...* will be best known for its inclusion of *Fairy Tale Of New York*, undoubtedly the most bizarre and heart warming Christmas song ever.

Using Kirsty MacColl, who was married to Lillywhite, as the female counter point was an inspired move and few people remained unmoved when confronted with Shane crooning as only he can 'I could have been someone' only to hear MacColl, in the exasperated voice of a partner who has heard it all before and refuses to go along with it sneer back, 'well so could anyone, you took my dreams for me/when I first met you'.

In one almost throw-away line MacGowan, wittingly or not, had just said more about the loss of hope, despair and general misery of someone on the streets who can still remember what it was like to dream.

A hundred homilies, worthy newspaper articles or earnest lectures may teach us about the plight of the homeless. They will not, however convince us of the plight of the individual and 'The Homeless' will be seen as an amorphous mass that appeared on the streets giving us a collective duty to get them out of sight. MacGowan deals with it on an individual level enabling us to experience the emotions and sympathise or even empathise with the subject. That is what makes MacGowan's songs so frequently brilliant.

The fact that he writes about the individual and not the phenomenon, be it homelessness, alcoholism or prostitution, gives to his songs an empathy that cannot come out of mere good intentions. This talent of appearing to write from within the eye of the storm is what sets him apart from other socially conscious songwriters and it goes back to his earliest days, vis; *The Old Main Drag*.

He spoke about this in an early interview with *Hot Press* in 1986 and said, 'it is a warning, you might as well say it: watch out. Piccadilly – that is where all the vice and drugs go on. Someone comes to London from anywhere, the north of England, Scotland, Ireland, expecting to make money and ending up totally fucked up. It happens to millions of people. I used to hang around there, yeah, but at least at the end of the day I could go home. Some of the kids came from far away and they could not get back. They ended up totally screwed up'.

Coming from anybody else these would have sounded like the words of a dilettante. But even though he had spent a term at Westminster you are never likely to class him as an ex-public school boy who got off on the danger and squalor of Kings Cross and 'the dilly'.

According to some of his friends he would have felt more at home there than in many other places.

As Madeline Sieler says, 'there is a natural sense of loneliness and melancholy in Shane and he is not comfortable when around people who want to hear him because of the fact that he is in a band or he is a star. He is much more relaxed with people who are not going to embarrass him by being too nice'.

When remarks like that are put in context you can understand the empathy he feels with the down-trodden people and the marginalised of society and the contempt that he feels for the roller coaster in which he, as a star, (whether he likes it or not that is, one facet of what he is) is occasionally obliged to take a ride.

Fairy Tale Of New York stunned many people who, with only a cursory knowledge of the band had presumed Shane to be a drunken, scrawny lout with bad teeth and a desire to give the Irish a bad name.

Here, he proved himself to be funny, perceptive and above all, a bloody good singer.

With the finest video of the year to accompany it and extensive airplay, what had seemed destined to be the most unlikely Christmas number one of all time was kept off the top spot only by The Pet Shop Boys and their risible cover of *Always On My Mind*.

9

THICK WORDS ON THIN ICE

' There were six men in Birmingham and in Guildford there's four / that were picked up and tortured and framed by the law / and the filth got promotion but they're still doing time / for being Irish in the wrong place at the wrong time / ...You'll be counting years, first five then ten / growing old in a lonely hell / 'round the yard and the stinking cell / from wall to wall and back again *(The Birmingham Six).*'

The most eagerly anticipated performance of Shane's new persona was the Fleadh Festival in London in June of 1994. The Fleadh had been a spiritual, musical, and cultural home for The Pogues given that it was a celebration of Irishness in London. In many ways the Fleadh was more important for people of Irish stock who had never been to Ireland but who felt that this was the perfect time to assert the identity which had been so important to their upbringing. The Fleadh was, and remains, a vital and essential expression of identity in the face of strangeness and, as a lot of those present would testify, hostility.

It is hard at times for those who have been born and bred in Ireland to appreciate what it actually means to be Irish. In much the same way that working-class Irish kids have adopted the identity of the teak tough Afro-American rapper or the suave, sophisticated Robert de Niro image of the Italian mobster, British born Irish children hold onto their aspirations and beliefs of what it is to be quintessentially Irish.

Ironically, this has been exploited by certain indigenous Irish groups, be it the Wolfe Tones singing *The Men Behind The Wire* for the weepy older generations of Irish emigrants who remember Ireland as a country that was still festering in the aftermath of a civil war, or their children who are fed lies by bands such as the Saw Doctors who speak of mythical parish oriented hurling matches and convent girls who might smile at you at Sunday Mass.

Musically and morally, these have been the two greatest crimes perpetrated on a weak and willing Irish emigrant underclass who have understandably grabbed on to some form of identification with the 'old country', no matter how fallacious.

But a quick read between the lines of such cultural fabrications, however, would lead most sober observers to see these acts, and others to be charlatans. While they might provide some sense of pseudo-solidarity and belonging, at the end of the night they are no more a valid representation of what it is to be part of an Irish underclass than the ridiculous image of the black rapper is of the black man or the image of the church-going, mother-loving, psychopath mobster is of the Italians.

What makes MacGowan's song writing so special is that he does not sing of a home with pictures of John Fitzgerald Kennedy, the Pope or de Valera on the wall, he sings of having no home at all. He sings of fleeing such pathetic mental ghettos and of making your own way in the world, with a kind thought for the older generation who might harbour such misconceptions but which mean nothing to the immigrant who has grown up working on a building site as a navvy or in a hospital as a doctor.

But while it is easy and erroneous to bestow the mantle of philosopher and spokesperson on his shoulders it is all too easy to forget that MacGowan is in the business of entertaining and, as a performer, he likes to cause controversy. This was shown yet again when he belatedly took the stage in Finsbury Park and half way through *The Woman Has Driven Me To Drink* he adopted what initially appeared to be a Sieg Heil salute.

Mary Coughlan played that day and more than most she would like to believe the rumours that he is a rehabilitated character. Any fears that the rumours were without foundation were realised when she saw him.

'He was absolutely wrecked that day', she says. 'He threw up over himself and had to be cleaned off before he went on stage, it was absolutely ridiculous. The band looked really pissed off with him because they had been rehearsing very hard and they don't need that kind of shit, it really was like the Shane of the bad old days'. But why does he do it?

This was grist to the tabloid mill. Despite the fact that he has sung about 'fucking black shirts' people still thought he was trying to pull a David Bowie (when, in an effort to promote his 1975 album *Station To Station* he gave a Nazi salute outside Earls Court).

A statement was released saying that what had appeared to be a Nazi salute was in fact, an 'old Gaelic form of greeting' in fact a "Tiochaidh Ar La" sign (Our Day Will Come).

While few people will argue that the modern day 'freedom fighters' of the north who have adopted the old Irish Republican Brotherhood slogan show as little respect or love for human life as the Nazis it was yet another example of the misrepresentation of a man who has always been an irritant to the British establishment, especially during the time he said that British soldiers in the North were legitimate targets.

In an interview with the English music magazine *Melody Maker*, Shane was steered onto the topic of politics and, while talking about Northern Ireland and British soldiers said, 'if you are carrying a gun, if you are prepared to shoot someone, you've got to be prepared to die yourself'.

While there is a certain basic logic in the statement, it was said in November of 1989, almost exactly two years after Enniskillen bombing in which 11 people were killed and had been greeted with universal revulsion by people from every walk of life, creed and political viewpoint.

MacGowan was quick to condemn the Enniskillen bombings but by then it was a case of too little too late and he was quickly rounded on by Tory MPs, in particular Terry Dicks and Geoffrey

Dickens (who in the latter part of 1994 condemned the issues of incest, rape, murder and homosexuality being dealt with on television, saying, in an admirable imitation of your average ostrich, that they did not reflect real life, said that MacGowan was 'a yob' and that he should be banned from the BBC.

Of course, what they really meant when they called him a 'yob' was that he was an Irish 'yob'. Paul McCartney had, after all, written the well meaning but naive *Give Ireland Back To The Irish* and while the song was not played on the radio there were not the same squeals of righteous indignation from the Tories as when an Irishman expressed a view about his own country.

The Pogues were tailor made to fall foul of the censors. Following the British governments decision to enact a similar version of Section 31, the radio programmers at the IBA, the body which issues the guidelines for all the UK's independent radio stations, decreed that their controversial *Birmingham Six* was too sensitive to be played. What was curious was that the song said nothing more inflammatory about the Birmingham Six than such figures as Cardinal Jenkins and Roy Hattersley, the Home Secretary had said at the time.

As Phil Chevron said at the time, 'the point is that we say it emotively. And if you say it with that type of emotion, it has much greater impact on people than if you say it with a bottle of claret in front of you'.

Manager Frank Murray was eager at the time to stress that the banning of the song represented a wider issue of civil liberties for all UK minority groups.

It was a point that Chevron concurred with, 'it is all part of how this government works. Section 28 was quite an easy number for them to use gay people as a starting point for legislation that can be extended to everybody else, to infringe on the rights of other so called minorities. They go for the easy targets then they spread their wings'.

Responding to criticism of the IBA's controversial decision to keep The Birmingham Six off their airwaves, the IBA's press officer, Stuart Patterson waffled, 'we are not calling it a ban. We pointed out to the Independent Local Radio stations the inadvisability of playing the song in the light of the Home Secretary's new broadcasting directives. When the Home Secretary's proscription was announced, we didn't immediately draw up a blacklist – we wrote to the stations informing them of the situation and asked if they had any doubts about the suitability of material they should consult with the IBA who would then give a ruling. Radio Piccadilly in Manchester sent us a list of five songs for examination – Paul McCartney's *Give Ireland Back To The Irish*, Stiff Little Fingers *Wasted Life*, That Petrol Emotions' *Terrorism*, U2's *Sunday Bloody Sunday* and The Pogues' song. The content of the other four was passed as suitable for broadcast'.

According to Patterson, The Pogues track was not rejected because it called into question the validity of The Birmingham Six and The Guildford Four verdicts, the problem arose because of the IBA's interpretation that it goes on to suggest that all Irish people are at a disadvantage in any dealings they might have with the British legal system. That blanket condemnation is unacceptable and might be seen to elicit support for organisations that have been proscribed by the Home Secretary.

Stuart Patterson responded to Frank Murrrays argument that the 'ban' had wide spread implications for civil liberties, that it in fact represented an infringement of the right of minorities to express legitimately held grievances.

'If that is all it had done, expressed doubts about a particular case, I would agree that there could be a problem', the press officer replied, 'but The Pogues were spreading their net beyond minority issues. There is a big difference between simply questioning a legal judgement and making a statement saying that if you are Irish you are likely to be arrested and convicted under the British Legal system.'

While there is a certain crude logic to his assertion that 'If you are carrying a gun... you've got to be prepared to die yourself', it was a good example of a musician getting involved in politics and muddling the facts. While there is no doubt that any man who dons a uniform and a gun and then patrols what can only be described as hostile territory can be nothing other than a target this was seen as a sort of endorsement of the IRA.

Unfortunately he was unaware of the real facts of the matter, and they were that the pre-ceasefire IRA were seen by a large percentage of the nationalist population as aggressors rather than defenders.

True, the knee cappings they administered, are only the inevitable extension of what the Sinn Fein courts did seventy years ago, but the IRA are also the leading criminal fraternity in their own community, using protection rackets, video piracy and, it is alleged, drug smuggling, although that has never been conclusively proved.

Therein lies the problem for any performer who makes even the most innocent remark on a contentious issue. Making the valid point that soldiers are there to shoot and be shot at can easily mislead the people who look on the likes of MacGowan as a commentator, when he is neither aware nor properly briefed on the facts, to make adequate pronouncements.

10
CHRISTY MOORE

It was fitting that one of the voices defending Shane was that of Christy Moore. No stranger to controversy himself (his song about Bobby Sands caused uproar when it was released), he had served a long and hard apprenticeship and was now enjoying success without forgetting where he had come from.

He has recorded three of Shane's songs, *Aislinn, A Pair Of Brown Eyes* and most famously, *A Fairy Tale Of New York*.

Moore can not remember exactly when he met MacGowan, recalling only that, 'I seemed to have been aware of him from early in his career, if not from his time with the Nips, certainly from his time with Pogue Mahone.'

'It was vitally important that someone like Shane came along when he did, it was important that his generation had a songwriter of the calibre of Shane to show that so called traditional and folk music was still valid and relevant to a younger audience, that it wasn't something you had to wear an aran jumper and a beard to like.' One of Shane's staunchest Irish colleagues was Christy Moore. Moore had spent twenty-five years ploughing his own furrow and became immensely popular for it. Known by many as the writer of amusing quasi-sagas such as *Lisdoonvarna* he was also highly respected in folk circles, having spent years playing the folk clubs in Ireland and Britain. He respects MacGowan because, 'he made traditional music relevant to a younger audience, he also brought a renewed strength vigour to the whole thing'.

'Music has to constantly reassess and re-evolve itself, music can't just stay static all the time, and when Shane brought in his punk sensibilities and background and mixed that with a trad upbringing it made something altogether new.'

Moore found the whole Noel Hill debacle to be quite laughable, 'look, Noel is a musician who has played with loads of different people, from myself to Planxty and others, he is a jobbing musician and I could never really figure out what he was trying to achieve when he had a go at Shane and The Pogues. Maybe they should have offered him a gig with them, then he might have changed his tune a bit!'.

While Moore admits that he is an avid fan, he falls short of actually putting any spurious label on the man and his work, and is wary of some of the hyperbole that has surrounded him.

'Genius, for instance, is a very vague, nebulous term and in many ways it really means very little in this particular context, it's not a very helpful term. What do I know? All I know is that he is my favourite contemporary Irish singer, I think that he is a startling talent and he touches my heart in a way that few, if any other singers of a similar style do.'

While a lot of people have made the easy comparison between MacGowan and Kelly, Moore is dismissive of these, saying that if anything, MacGowan has more to offer.

'To be honest with you, Luke was a singer but he never wrote a song. He would interpret songs and I suppose he made some of the songs his own in a certain way but certainly I think it is all a bit too easy to compare the two because they both liked to drink, there is a gulf of real difference between the two.'

Do you think that the image of the hard drinking, hard living Shane was manipulated by those around him or was something that he deliberately milked?

'I think there is a certain extent to which Shane may have camped things up a bit because it is a very easy persona to hide behind, it means that people are happy dealing with the public layer and get enough to satisfy them there without scratching underneath and maybe finding out about the real person submerged underneath. Every time that I have met Shane, be it in a television studio, or around at gigs and things, he has always been fairly well on and and he has admitted himself that it has been more than just drink for a long time.

'I can understand and empathise with that, I went through a period where I genuinely believed that I could not function without the crutch of one drug or another, be it drink or different drugs. Of course, this is rubbish but it is a very difficult rut to try and get out of and maybe Shane just never really wanted to get out of it badly enough. People have often wondered about what he would do if he was clean and sober, but anything like that is idle conjecture and maybe there is a certain point about drink being a vital part of his writing.'

But even if purely from his health point of view, do you not feel that the people around him should have helped Shane out more than they actually did?

'All of this really isn't for me to comment on, I think that it is largely a smoke screen that is used to cloud the fact that Shane is such a brilliant songwriter, but yeah, all you can do is give love and support to someone who is in that type of predicament but there have to be people who bear a certain element of responsibility, maybe we are all guilty, maybe we should all have applied ourselves to trying to help Shane more than we did.'

While there was no great surprise when Shane was fired from The Pogues there were people who felt that the band had, if not deliberately, then unconsciously, used Shane for all he was worth and let him go when it was obvious that there was going to be no good from him for a long time.

'It obviously got to the stage where Shane just had to go, for the good of himself and for the good of everybody else, there was really nothing good to be achieved in him staying any longer.

'It is no reflection on the band that he had to go, it is just that he was in one room for long enough and he decided that it was time to move on to a different room. A lot of people make the same old mistake of staying with something for longer than they should and just making a mockery of the whole thing.

'It is very difficult to keep the enthusiasm and energy going for twenty years, the way it happened with Luke Kelly for example, there is no way that I personally could cope with a situation like that. I think that it's very unhealthy. It is no reflection on the other guys in the band, the rest of The Pogues are great guys and great musicians but I think the time had come for Shane to get out while he still could.'

Do you think that there is a future for Shane and his music?

'Well, Jesus, I would hope so, I think that he is an absolutely amazing talent that has graced us with some of the best songs of his generation, I can't say how strongly I admire the man and so obviously one hopes that he will come back with a great album, but maybe it is time for him to go to something else. Maybe he should try something else for a while but I do hope that he continues to be creative because he has touched a lot of people, the way he has written about emigration and other things without ever descending into cliché he really is a phenomenal song writer.'

Would you go along with the accepted view that 'Fairy Tale Of New York' is probably the greatest Christmas song ever?

'I don't actually because I don't actually think that 'Fairy Tale Of New York' is just a Christmas song, in fact I think that it puts unnecessary limits on the song to confine to merely a Christmas song. The imagery in the song is absolutely dazzling and the Christmas context is one image that is used, but there is a whole array there to choose from. I think that it is just a very human song, that deals with relationships in a very special way.

'That is actually what makes the song so hard to cover with any real meaning, I found it probably one of the hardest songs I have ever tried to do.'

MacGowan in Dublin 1993 – the only problem with a broken arm is trying to hold two pints and light a fag at the same time.

MacGowan does bis bit man impression in Finsbury Park 1994.

Shane MacGowan, Christy Moore and Tommy Byrne of The Wolfe Tones at the reception for The Siamsa Cois Laoi.

Shane MacGowan and Matt Dillion, New York 1986.

Shane in Wonderland. The SFX 1986.

'I know I left my keys around here somewhere,' Finsbury Park 1994.

'Are you looking at my beer?' Dublin 1994.

The long hair and beard of 1993 was a far cry from the punk aesthetic of 1977.

The Ierne Club 1990. The Pogues and The Dubliners take a break from recording one of the many football songs of that year, 'Jacks Heroes'.

Supporting U2 in Croke Park in 1987; the Padre Pio laminate has now become a collectors item.

MacGowan, looking tired and worn in Dublin, September 1994.

Joe Strummer and Shane 1990.

Shane in the Point, Christmas 1988.

More crimes against fashion, Christmas 1989.

Mean and Moody. Shane in 1990.

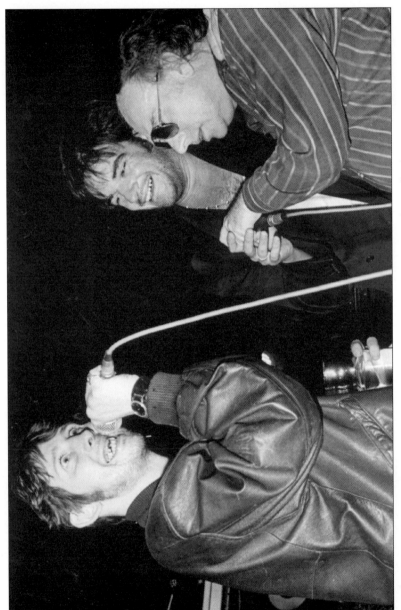

Shane, Van Morrison and Fiachna of the Hot House Flowers live it up.

11
Not a Wonderful World

With Shane now out of The Pogues there was considerable doubt as to whether he would continue in music in any form whatsoever. His sacking had precipitated a further decline in his health, and his continued use of drugs led many observers to worry about his future. At this stage it was not so much whether he would record again but whether he would live to see out the next year.

His appearances around London had shown him to be a pale shadow of his former self. His shambling incoherence while talking and increasingly shabby demeanour did not bode well for the future. The man who had written some of the most touching and evocative songs of the previous ten years seemed to be gone forever, only to be replaced by yet another rock and roll casualty, a tragic testament to the pit falls of the music business and a warning to younger kids that while drink and soft drugs will play hell with your physical and mental health, hard substances will destroy it.

What was most disturbing was the fact that it didn't seem to bother him. A couple of aborted sojourns in the odd health clinic weren't going to save him, and with whatever safety net The Pogues had provided for him now gone, it was going to take something special to stop him ending up dead in a toilet somewhere with a needle stuck in his arm.

It was particularly fitting that Shane should find a much needed ally at this time in the form of Nick Cave. Cave had, like MacGowan, cut his musical teeth during the punk wars. The stick-like figure had arrived in London from Australia in the mid-seventies and his performances with his seminal first band, The

Birthday Party, and their aggressive, chaotic activities soon placed Cave at the forefront of the new movement. After the prog-rock sloth of the seventies, young, aggressive and nihilistid gunsligers such as Cave were absolutely compelling.

Eventually, inevitably, they imploded but it was only the beginning for Cave, who even in the midst of all the madness of the time had displayed a keen lyrical awareness and startling use of imagery that far surpassed that of his contemporaries. Like MacGowan, a lot of his work bore an almost literary quality, and it was no surprise when his first novel, *And The Ass Saw the Angel* was published in 1992 by Faber and Faber.

Like MacGowan, it was fairly obvious to any observer that while Cave may have moved in the punk world, he was not exactly in it. They shared an interest in melodies and in the nature and history of music. Their exceptional lyrical ability which set them aside from the vast majority of their peers who had hopped on the punk band wagon out of love for the sheer exuberance of the noise and a craving for the buzz, chemical and otherwise, that punk provided.

Like MacGowan, Cave had gone beyond the wraps of speed that helped to fuel the punk movement. While Cave may have sneered at the indolence of the 'sixties, he was quite prepared to indulge in their favoured drug, acid. After the break-up of The Birthday Party, Cave moved to Berlin where his lyrics displayed his continuing fascination with controlled substances.

Many of the lyrics from that time are peppered with the nightmarish tone of a writer who had gone beyond mere curiosity about drugs.

If anything Cave explored darker territory than MacGowan, who tended to be more subtle and introverted in his writing. Cave, with gallows humour and love for the theatrical gesture often catered to Grand Guignol sentiments at the expense of a tune.

Like MacGowan, Cave had soon graduated from tripping to indulging in Heroin and this had blunted a lot of his creativity during the early to mid 'eighties. Many fans and critics feared that Cave would blow his undeniably considerable talent just to become yet another bloated smack-head, occasionally rearing his head from opium dreams to send some demented missive from the edge of whatever hell he was residing in at the time.

But while his habit undoubtedly caused havoc in his private and professional life, Cave had developed a similar gift to Shane's in that both had the ability to confront their own personal heart of darkness and still manage to convey their feelings in a form of music which provided them with a valuable cathartic outlet. This outlet also gave the world some of the most compelling, stark, and beautiful music of the last ten years.

The release in 1990 of his fourth album, *The Good Son* was a welcome return to form and a vindication of Cave the songwriter, while the release two years later of *Henry's Dream* had cemented Cave's position as one of the most graphic, literate and intense songwriters of his generation. But while he was quite happy to sing about 'a fag in a whale bone corset draping his dick across my cheek' (*Papa Won't Leave You Henry*), he had developed the tender side of his writing that showed a growing maturity and ease with life, and as he said himself in numerous interviews, the birth of his son Luke had infused him with renewed sensitivity. Coupled with a more global view of things than he had had before, he felt that he had grown up somewhat.

Cave had frequently expressed admiration for MacGowan and the two were to go on and become quite good friends.

The announcement in late October of 1993 that MacGowan and Cave were to join forces for a Christmas release was greeted with a mixture of anticipation and bemusement by most observers.

While the two of them had long expressed an interest in writing and recording together, and it was a thought that had many people salivating at the prospect. Shane had already written what was arguably the greatest Christmas song ever in *Fairy Tale Of New York* and surely it would be expecting too much of the newly formed duo to try and top that. They didn't, for shortly after the announcement that they were to collaborate on a single it emerged that they were to do a take on that perennial favourite, the Louis Armstrong number, *What A Wonderful World*.

This, people thought, was more like it. Would two of the darkest songwriters in music do a wonderfully ironic and post-modern version of a song that, while written in a sombre enough mood, had become the preserve of sherry-sodden spinsters at Christmas parties, or would they do a straight version with no frills as a simple tribute?

Their debut performance of the song was scheduled for *Later With Jools Holland*, the best music program on BBC and the ideal, informal setting for such an unusual pairing. What followed can be politely described as something of a disappointment. Or less politely as a disaster. Cave and MacGowan played it straight and while their decision not to do some sort of smarmy version of a song they both obviously admired was commendable, the version they inflicted on the world made a mockery of one's sense of anticipation. Perched precariously on two stools, and with MacGowan wearing a pair of aviator shades to hide his eyes from the viewers, the pair had all the appeal of two drunks sitting on a park bench in Camden at three o' clock in the morning.

Shane in particular looked to be in a bad way and it was nothing short of pathetic to see what had once been an awesome talent reduced to be carried along in the song by Cave, who was never regarded as being the best of singers anyway. The song finished to muted applause from the assembled studio throng of fellow musicians and a few invited guests. What should have been a genuinely exciting moment in recent music history had fizzled out and become a sad parody of what could have been.

On the short lived RTE youth program, *Electric Ballroom*, MacGowan and Cave were interviewed in the rather predictable setting of a smoky pub and an obviously ropy Shane seemed to be in as bad a way as when he had left the Pogues two years earlier. If anything, he seemed worse, and yet again we had an example of Shane being coaxed into doing a broadcast interview when he should have been off somewhere getting some much needed help for his ever worsening physical and mental condition. Like so many people before them, the producers of *Electric Ballroom* had decided to go ahead and interview him when the most helpful thing they could have done would have been to give him the taxi fare home. While you can't expect them to apply any morality to their job, it begged the question again as to what his management was doing letting him be interviewed in such a bad state.

In yet another rambling, virtually incoherent performance it seemed as if Shane had lost all interest in his music. Saying that he had no time for fame and the adulation of people who admired his music, he claimed that he was only interested in the financial rewards that his music brought, 'because with money I can have a good time, you know, and that is what I am interested in at the end of the day'.

Such candour from a pop star, even a reluctant one, would ordinarily be extremely refreshing but coming on the back of the disappointing duet with Cave these words were more reminiscent of a punch-drunk boxer who was out to get one last pay day before retiring into feeble and impotent obscurity.

12
HOW NOT TO DO AN INTERVIEW

In over fifteen years of national broadcasting, Dave Fanning has been responsible for some of the most amazing interviews ever transmitted over the air waves. Be it an obviously ropy Willie DeVille, an irritable Nick Cave or an interview conducted in the buff with U2 (seldom has a nation breathed such a sigh of relief that they were listening to radio and not looking at television), each interview is liable to throw up something new and exciting.

Probably the most embarrassing of these interviews went out on 22 November 1988 when The Pogues (Shane and Philip, later joined by Terry Woods) and Mary Coughlan arrived in the studio after being at the press launch for the *If I Should Fall From The Grace Of God* album. The guests had obviously indulged rather too lavishly in the free beer that goes with such events.

Coughlan had a reputation for liking booze that was nearly as well-documented as Shane's, and so it was no surprise when they came on sounding a bit worse for wear, but when Mary's first words were 'shut the fuck you' it was obvious that the listeners were going to enjoy an interview that would have an increasingly nervous and irritated host sounding obviously cheesed off before long.

DAVE FANNING Does that mean that you will be playing more than just the one date in Ireland?

PHIL CHEVRON No, we will be doing the King's Hall in Belfast as well.

DF   You're not going to do lots of little dates around the country like you did the last time?

PC   No, because we lost money on that.

DF   How did it go in the States since the last time I saw you, you didn't lose money on that did you, because you had to play lots of small little places?

PC   Well, we didn't make very much. Let's put it this way, the only place we lose money in is Ireland.

SHANE MacGOWAN No, no, we lose money everywhere.

MARY COUGHLAN I must say at this point in time that I did some Pogues-type gigs last St Patrick's day... in the Brixton Academy and we did the Town And Country for three nights and I just had a ball.

DF   And when you say that you had a good time were you getting up on stage and singing with The Pogues or were you playing beforehand or what?

MC   I sang a couple of songs with Shane and then Kirsty would get up and do a few, and I think by the end of the night there were about seventeen people on stage.

PC   Twenty-two actually, it was like a Celtic black soul revue.

MC   It was just lovely and it was like this big,.. big, big gig and we were throwing flowers all over the place and it was lovely.

DF   Well those gigs that happened in London around St Patrick's Day, they have been captured on two different ways on video.

PC   Captured is the only way to put it.

DF   One of them is a documentary type thing and one of them is a live performance. So were you happy with the finished product?

PC   You can never be happy with the way you see yourself on the screen, to be honest, but other people seem quite pleased.

MC   You get really embarrassed when you see your big fat face on the screen.

Embarrassed was the operative word the next day. Having continued in that vein for nearly the whole show it was, as has been mentioned, interesting radio, but even then it was interesting in a prurient sense. Shane sounded as if he was talking with a bucket over his head he was so drunk. Slurring away, the greatest contribution he made to the conversation was to crack open cans of beer and make strange hissing noises into the microphone. We were witnessing what appeared to be total self-destruction live on air, the complete unravelling of two of our greatest performers in a drunken frenzy which saw them in such a state that they would never have been allowed into a club, let alone get involved in a live studio debate. Here we witnessed a bunch of people in the aftermath of a booze frenzy and talking the type of drink-sodden rubbish that everybody has uttered at some stage or another, but seldom has it been beamed out to a nation courtesy of Fab 2FM.

Yet again we had what seemed to be Shane playing into the hands of those who sought to discredit him.

Regardless of any lofty ideals MacGowan might have had regarding self-preservation and even simply trying to stay together so as not to look like an asshole when he went on air, Fanning himself deserved a bit more respect.

He had been good to The Pogues and had, as usual, been a voice of reason when other people were getting hysterical about the whole Pogues issue. Come on, he seemed to be saying, it's only music after all.

The embarrassment and awkwardness in his voice was palpable when he was talking to them. He tried to keep the conversation between himself and Phil Chevron as much as possible but that was virtually impossible between Shane's incoherent interruptions and Mary's drunken jokes.

The sense of frustration spread to Chevron himself when Mary said 'Motherfucker' for the second time in as many minutes. He could obviously feel the whole gig being blown from right underneath him. But even Fanning (with what sounded like barely maintained restraint and seriously gritted teeth) who has dealt with some of the most notoriously difficult interviewees in his time, found it difficult to get anything approaching sense from the guests.

The question has to be asked, why were they allowed to go on the show and be interviewed in the first place? God knows it wouldn't be the first time a musician or a band turned up for an interview too 'out of their minds' to make it worthwhile. Indeed it was not the first time that Shane himself had turned up in no fit state for an interview, and usually the planned item is quietly scrapped and a substitute item inserted in its place.

This is, after all, Shane MacGowan we are talking about, he himself has said that he cannot remember the last time he was totally sober so it would not take a genius of a producer or a presenter to have some back-up prepared.

Ian Wilson, the series producer of the Fanning show was manning the controls that night which makes it even more surprising that the debacle was allowed to continue. But, says Wilson, 'we knew what we were dealing with when we planned to have them in the studio but they gave no indication as to how wrecked they really were when they arrived so we just got on with the show. It was only as the show progressed that I realised just how drunk they really were but at that stage there really is nothing you can actually do.

'You certainly can't pull them after they have actually gone on air because it is too late by then and you just tend to make a bad situation even worse. It would have exacerbated all the problems we already had if we turned around five minutes into the show and told them that they were being pulled off, there would have been war.'

The whole affair was made even worse by the fact that Fanning has a lot of time for Shane, 'I think he is an incredibly talented guy, he has written some fine tunes. Having said that, I get a bit suspicious when people start saying that he is a genius, certainly a lot of what he has written bears the mark of greatness, but if anyone wants to listen to a genius I will sit them down in a room and play them a bunch of Randy Newman records.

'I couldn't believe it when I realised how bad they all were, they had just been to a gig and they must have been lashing the pints down at an incredible rate. I knew what Shane was like, of course. I had interviewed him after the Self Aid concert and he was pretty well gone then as well. You hear all these stories as well, of course. You know what this business is like, you do something and it gets magnified and blown out of all proportion, but I had heard even from an early stage that he was taking crazy amounts of acid and stuff like that'.

The memory of the whole incident is still enough to make Mary Coughlan wince. 'Oh, Jesus, you heard that as well', was her reaction when I brought it up.

'I wasn't even supposed to be on the show that night, but we had been at the video reception for the Paddy's Day Gig and I was drunk, so when Shane asked me if I wanted to go on the radio with him I jumped at the chance.

'By that stage of course we were all well jarred and I was as bad as any of them. It was probably one of the most embarrassing things that I have ever done, I can tell you.

'Ian Wilson was absolutely furious and I can't blame him. We were in an awful state, I still feel sorry for poor Dave. Jesus, he really had his work cut out for him that night I can tell you. I had to write a letter of apology to RTE afterwards, that was how badly they took it. If I hadn't written that letter I don't think that I would ever have got back onto the station in any capacity at all. They were that pissed off about the whole thing, and as I said I can't really blame them.'

What about Shane, did he have to write a similar letter? 'As far as I know Shane was kind of expected to do something similar but you know Shane, as far as I know he never bothered his arse, it isn't really the type of thing that he would take the time out to do. I dunno, maybe Frank (Murray, manager of The Pogues) did, I'm not sure'.

Surely Frank should have stopped you all, particularly Shane, from going on to the show in the first place?

'Yeah, well, there were a lot of things Frank should have done, you know what I'm saying?'.

Coughlan's friendship with Shane continued when he moved into a house in Bray near where she lived.

'He was his usual self, he would go the local pubs and have a few pints and things, no big deal.'

The last time she saw Shane was at the Fleadh in Finsbury Park. 'Jesus, he was awful', she recalls. 'He arrived late for the gig and he was in bits; a really bad state. There was no way he should have played, he got sick on Vince Power before he went on and everything, it has just got to the stage where nobody is laughing anymore, something is going to give sooner or later. I know people have been saying that about him for years but he does seem to look genuinely worse than he has done. He is that bit older now as well, it will be harder for him to recuperate.

'I don't know how he kept it up, I was like that myself for a while as well, but I had to give it up for the kids sake but Jaysus, I am glad I did because you can't last at that pace forever. It is a bit pathetic as well, you know. People look at you and think, "fuck, can you not get it together at all?", you know, "who do you think you are?" that type of thing, and they are right. Especially when you go on tour and it can get very gruelling when you are on the road for a long time, you just have to try and look after yourself, and getting skulled to the extent that Shane has done, so frequently, is not going to help you any.'

When told that MacGowan's single, *The Church Of The Holy Spook* was something of a disappointment, she was not surprised, 'Jaysus, if he can't change he should maybe give it up, for his own sake, because he is just such a lovely guy'.

13
FROM ROTTEN TO ROWLAND

While MacGowan may be the most obvious songwriter of recent times to draw heavily on his Irishness, he is by no means the only one in recent years to use the emigrant experience to fuel some of his material. From Johnny Rotten to Madness, Kevin Rowland to Morrissey, the influence of Irish stock should not be underestimated.

Before the emergence of John Lydon, punk was nothing more than a proto-style formulated by two art school dilettantes, Malcolm McLaren and Vivienne Westwood. Fuelled by situationist slogans and bondage gear, the whole early punk scene was nothing more than something to do for a couple of bored middle class fashion victims.

The introduction of Rotten into The Sex Pistols brought a whole new infusion of that vicious anger and furious nihilism that was to become quintessentially punk. This was no designer attitude from Lydon – although he grew up in a typical working class house in Islington in North London, one of his earliest memories is 'of the stale smell of bacon and cabbage, that perennial Irish meal'.

His tale was one of classic disenfranchisement. Alienated from the society of his birthplace because of his parents' background, he was deemed a stranger in their homeland too because of his funny, nasal whine and bad attitude. The burgeoning scene that was punk at the time was the perfect outlet for the young Rotten and other citizens of the 'no future' generation, kids who hated the music played by their big brothers, kids who were sick to the teeth of outmoded 'sixties platitudes.

Who better to act as a conduit for this anger than Rotten, a young man alienated from not one but two societies. Lydon subsequently made a very lucrative career out of replicating that anger and his auto-biography, *No Irish, No Blacks, No Dogs* is one of the most vitriolic and entertaining books about music to be released in recent years.

Interestingly enough, the young Shane MacGowan, who was just finding his feet at the time, comes in for some of the famous Rotten contempt; 'I remember playing one gig and Shane MacGowan was there at the front, pog-ing around at the top of the stage with everybody else, wearing a Union Jack tee-shirt. The next time I saw him he was at the front of the stage again but this time he called himself Shane O'Hooligan and he was wearing an Irish tee-shirt. I could never understand people who could switch their national identity like that, so quickly. I found it rather pathetic the way he did that and I did not have very much time for him when he was in the Pogues, either'.

While Lydon gives MacGowan short shrift for 'changing his identity' as he put it, it raises a very relevant point about MacGowan and how, from an early age, he was obviously trying to fit in. He would not be the first person to live in Britain and try to kick over the traces of his Irish roots (or indeed any number of ethnic backgrounds) in an effort to assimilate into the crowd and not be marked out. As Rotten himself admits, it was not a particularly good time to be Irish and living in London.

While Rotten was, in many ways, the voice of a generation in The Sex Pistols, other bands followed in their wake who might not have made as dramatic an impact but had as much to say, merely in different ways. Madness were the embodiment of a working-class fun band.

While bands such as Joy Division had emerged from the council estates of Manchester and produced some of the darkest (and most brilliant) music ever recorded, Madness came from the London equivalent of the council estates and dealt with more homely issues.

While the people who had fought the punk wars were now wallowing in Ian Curtis' self-loathing and ultimately, his self-destruction, their younger brothers' were getting off on the 'heavy, heavy, monster sound' of the self-styled nutty boys. A bunch of first and second generation Irish emigrant children, they were as confused as anyone else by the world around them but rather than snarl and snipe at their surroundings as Lydon had done they sublimated their anger through writing some of the most potent pop songs of that decade. They preferred to bunk off school and smoke a fag behind the bike sheds, while eyeing up the local talent, than to storm the gates of society and promote anarchy.

Arguably the greatest of these songwriters, was Kevin Rowland. The child of an Irish couple, he first announced his arrival with the 1981 album, *Searching For The Young Soul Rebels*. This masterful debut was one of the first new wave records to embrace a brass section and the biggest hit from the record, *Geno* was number one for two weeks.

Never the most prolific of writers, Rowland resisted the urge to release a quick follow-up and cement the success of his debut. He waited nearly three years before releasing the second.

Too Ray Aye was the first real indication of the importance of his Irish roots. In a style that was later to be copied by numerous crusty bands of the late eighties, Rowland incorporated fiddles and traditional Irish rhythms to even greater success than he had horns on his first album, and went on to have three hits in quick succession, the biggest being *Come On Eileen*, a triumphant espousal of teenage lust and the gang mentality of young lads. While the sound of that song has been aped by pale imitators such as the Bluebells, and other lesser talents, this still stands as one of the most life affirming singles of the eighties.

But it was, nonetheless, 'Oirish' rather than Irish, the silly clothes and complete change from his urban image of previous years always looked somewhat contrived, and while he doffed his cap to Van Morrison with a cover of *Jackie Wilson Said*, he never looked as comfortable as the Belfast bard did with the whole notion of the Celtic revival. This was largely to do with the fact that Rowland was trying to adopt an image which was false. That aspect of Irish culture was as alien to him as it was to young indigenous Irish people who felt embarrassed by the whole 'diddly-eye' movement.

He did not strike pay dirt until his third and, perversely, least successful album. *Don't Stand Me Down* is one of the most criminally under-rated albums of the last twenty years. Dealing with Rowland approaching his thirties and trying to come to terms with his childhood and upbringing, it saw him adopt a bizarrely conservative image of very proper suits and ties, and if he looked like a new age traveller on the previous album, he had now turned into what appeared to be an insurance salesman.

While his dress might have been conservative the music was anything but. In its own understated way, it was one of the most ground breaking and brave albums of the last few years, featuring as it does a six minute conversation between himself and his right-hand man and saxophonist Nicky Gatfield (now head of A&R at EMI London, strangely enough) which consisted of the two of them discussing Rowland's new girlfriend. The resulting chat was something you would be more likely to hear down in the pub rather than on a record and would appear to be the self indulgent rubbish of a man who admitted that he was never happy with the music business (the stories and rumours about Rowland's state of mind around the time of the recording and re-recording of this album would almost make a book in themselves).

But for some reason it works, particularly when Rowland then goes off into a bitchy tangent about 'the kind of people who wear creases in their old Levi's, the kind of people who say super and fabulous... I don't like these people, may I be clear on this point'. It was the kind of twist and observation that would be more akin to Elvis Costello than the man who had sang 'pull up that dress, my thoughts I confess, verge on dirty' on *Come On Eileen*.

This was a very different Rowland, however, visibly struggling to make sense of what he saw around him in Thatcher's Britain, where the optimism of his youth, of 'cheap love nights on the Edgware Road had been replaced by cheap cynicism and music 'that all sounds the same'.

He really gets to the heart of the matter when, on *Knowledge Of Beauty* he sings, 'how I swooned to your stories of Royal victories, your books of history were fairy tales to me'. That couplet alone is worth the price of the album as he tries to come to terms with Irishness and his age, and while musically this album was far removed from the material being released by The Pogues at around the same time, they could almost have been written by the same person.

While he must have known that the record was virtually guaranteed to be commercial suicide after the huge success and radio friendliness of its predecessor, it is a must for any record collection and in these revisionist times deserves to be reappraised and celebrated for the work of quirky genius that it is.

Of all the people that have compared to MacGowan, Rowland's name is never mentioned, yet both were of a similar age, from virtually identical backgrounds and drew from the same subject matter in equally cathartic ways. And while their careers were to follow widely divergent paths and their music was to sound completely different, there is a similar thread of integrity and shared experience common to the work of both men.

14

THE FINAL CHAPTER

'Rock and Roll you crucified me, left me all alone / I never should have turned my back on the old folks back at home' (*The Church Of The Holy Spook*)

Despite the pasting given to the single *The Church Of The Holy Spook* by some of the inkie press, the first single he had released in a couple of years was not a bad effort. But in many ways its very competence was half of its undoing. People expected to be surprised at what they heard but what they got was a song that could have been any number of old Pogues staples. A fast and pretty furious number, with too many lyrical twists and turns to say anything of any real importance, it seemed to flounder under its own weight and for all the lumbering enthusiasm it most definitely was not going to excite any but the most ardent Shane fan. This of course begged the question of whether there was such a thing left as an ardent Shane fan.

The success of The Pogues without Shane had proved that people were quite prepared to live without him. There is no doubt that he had been one of the greatest song writing talents of the last twenty years in any style of contemporary music, but pop stars (and like it or not, that was how he was seen), even ones as eloquent and unconventional as MacGowan, have a notoriously brief shelf-life. If they do not release an album every couple of years to remind the public of their existence, they are liable to disappear.

One of the worrying things for MacGowan was that many of the people who had maintained an interest in him during this fallow period were those professional ambulance chasers, the music press.

To them MacGowan had always been the perfect Irish Rebel who fulfilled their liberal expectations of what a modern day Celtic bard should be; brilliant, articulate, drunk, and at war with himself. Of course this would be denied by all but the most honest of these gentlemen of the British press but one can hardly blame them for their treatment of MacGowan given the fact that they had a ready-made story in The Pogues and their singer. All they had to do was to leave a tape recorder running and then submit the transcript. MacGowan was famous after all, for giving a good interview. One can hardly blame the British press if this situation inevitably resulted in garbled ideas and reinforced stereotypes, especially as the Irish press, who should have known better, had treated him much the same way.

Despite the largely hostile reception shown to *The Church Of The Holy Spook* by the music press, MacGowan's debut solo single was a competent enough effort. If anything, it was this mere competence that set critics teeth on edge. Nothing had been heard of the man since *What A Wonderful World* other than the occasional chaotic live appearance, but then, all of Shane's live appearances were chaotic and people had learned not to read too much into any craziness that might be witnessed there.

What the reviewers wanted was a record that was either going to prove that the talent which had written so many genuinely classic songs down the years was alive and burning as brightly as ever or that he had turned into some sort of Elvis O'Presley, a wasted buffoon whose demise was something to upset one – a tragic rock and roll waste – the usual cliché.

What they got was something else entirely. *For The Church Of The Holy Spook* was merely adequate. A standard rock workout in a sub-standard Clash style it was in the same vein as twenty such singles released and ignored every month, and if anything, it sounded too jaded even to be lumped in with the New Wave Of New Wave.

MacGowan had cheated the world by refusing to give them the opportunity to write their glowing obituaries, but he had also denied them their chance to hoist him upon their shoulders and hail the conquering hero for one last time. In short, he had denied them their story, and that annoyed them.

But while there is no denying that the sheer sense of anti-climax of the first release was more of a let-down than an actual real disappointment, there is no doubt that there are several songs on *The Snake* that stand up to anything that MacGowan has done before. There is no doubt that MacGowan's voice is showing signs of wear and tear, and on *A Mexican Funeral In Paris* he sounds as if he has been gargling with paraffin and small stones. But unlike many of his contemporaries who have affected such vocal traits, the songs are well suited to such treatment, and while there is nothing to match *Frank's Wild Years* or *Rain Dogs* on *The Snake*, he doesn't have to worry too much if his voice becomes even raspier.

The second single, *That Woman's Got Me Drinking* (it was during this song at the 1994 Fleadh that he caused the controversy) was an altogether better release. Featuring Johnny Depp on guitar, it is the type of song that The Golden Horde spent ten years trying to write and failed. It was premiered on *Top Of The Pops* on September 28 1994, and as with the previous live appearance he had made on that show with The Dubliners, he left an indelible mark.

The inclusion of Depp on the song surprised a lot of people, but the two had been hanging around London for about a year. Depp has made a career out of playing with marginalised figures, and he got to meet a real live one in MacGowan. At that time the only occasion MacGowan got mentioned in the papers was if he did or said something controversial, but even that was losing its appeal. With people like Kurt Cobain, Kristen Pfaff and even Bill Hicks dying within a few months of each other, MacGowan's apparent inability to kill himself, no matter how hard he tried, was no longer of any interest to the gossip column writers of the music press. Depp, on the other hand, was fascinated with this strange character who had, in classic cinema cliché speak, hidden depths.

While he gets a guitar credit on the album, Depp didn't play a major role in the song, but as MacGowan said, 'what he did play sounded really good'.

It seems a perfect symbiotic relationship. Ever since he escaped from the vacuous teen hell that was *21 Jump Street*, Johnny Depp had craved genuine credibility, and seen his roles grow from the standard fluff pieces to genuinely worthy efforts such as *Benny And Joon* and *What's Eating Gilbert Grape*. He was, of course, best known for *Edward Scissorhands*, and ever since he has looked for roles that disguise his looks and emphasise his talent.

This attitude also goes a long way to explaining why somebody like MacGowan would be so appealing to him. With a face that could contort itself into truly spectacularly ugly poses, and with teeth that were likened by one American journalist to tombstones ('some stand up straight, some lie to the side and some just aren't there at all'), he was a godsend to any young actor who wanted to get away from the superficiality of Hollywood and try and do something meaningful. To a man who is now going out with super-waif Kate Moss, MacGowan must have seemed like the Oracle of Delphi.

Of course, it suits MacGowan as well, because, try as he might, Depp still cannot completely shake off his young fan base, and their Top Of The Pops appearance was punctuated by the type of girlie shrieking that one doesn't usually hear when Shane MacGowan appears.

Amidst Whigfield and all the assorted pop fodder of the day, MacGowan and his band stormed through the song with an enthusiasm that bordered on the dangerous.

MacGowan stalked the stage with all the malice and hysteria of a deranged war veteran, which is what he must have looked like to the vast majority of the audience. But for all the implied chaos of his appearance he looked well, was in control, and if that performance does not propel him back into the nation's consciousness, then nothing will. The relieved voice of the inane presenter when she said, 'well, we told you anything could happen' spoke volumes.

One of the most interesting interviews that MacGowan has done since his 'come back' was with Jon Wilde in *Loaded* magazine. An experienced rock hack, Wilde had interviewed MacGowan before and knew well what to expect from as garrulous a character as Shane.

'I went to Filthy MacNasty's one night towards the end of August 1994', says Wilde. 'He seemed to be in a bad old way, actually. He was clearly either on something or coming off something, but that has been the way with Shane for so long now that it is difficult to tell when he is straight or when he is doped. He is a very hardy old soul, of course, but he has been living what amounts to a reality that is parallel to the rest of us for so long that I am surprised he can talk at all, to be honest with you'.

In the interview MacGowan talks of the years of excess which were followed by his years in the wilderness saying, 'I am not a healthy man. I have lived a totally irresponsible existence. I've given no thought to what I have swallowed or poured down my throat or put up my nose over the years. It was only when a doctor told me that I was running out of lives that I decided to calm down – purely for the sake of staying alive. I have had to adjust to a slower pace of life and that has made writing a lot more difficult'.

But while he admits that he has had to temper his legendary consumption of substances, both legal and otherwise, he is still unrepentant. 'If you are asking whether drink and drugs have worked for me, I have got to say that they have. I'm with William Blake on this one. Drink and drug and all that shit, it's a short cut to the subconscious. Y'know, real wisdom has got fuck-all to do with your three times tables and the capital of Belgium and all that bollocks. When you take a load of drugs, you get into a state where you see reality in a completely different light and that obviously helps when you are writing songs'.

This is hardly an original point, Hunter S Thompson virtually invented a whole new style of journalism with his Gonzo epics and no-holds-barred accounts of his pursuit for drugs, happiness and The American Dream. But while Thompson's work still remains undeniably brilliant and often embarrassingly funny (try reading *Fear And Loathing In Las Vegas* on a bus without laughing aloud), the figure he cuts these days is pathetic. One of the saddest sights of the last few years was when he contributed to the programme celebrating the twenty-fifth anniversary of *Rolling Stone* magazine. He was desperately sad. Like MacGowan, he claims to have cut down his consumption of drugs, but like MacGowan, he is left with a permanent slur. MacGowan would do well to look at him and see what is one of the most stark examples of how nobody gets away with doing what they have done.

With quotes such as, 'I have had to adjust to a slower pace of life and that makes writing a lot more difficult', and the evidence of the single that had been released, it was difficult to hold out much hope for the quality of the album. But while the *The Church Of The Holy Spook* was unremarkable, there are several songs included on *The Snake* that deserve to be considered among the best songs he has ever written.

Most notably of these is the third track, *The Song With No Name* which is genuinely breathtaking in its sheer emotional rawness, and is unquestionably one of the finest songs MacGowan has ever written. Indeed, it is unlikely that he have could have written a song like that a few years ago, the sense of regret infused in the song obviously deals with the last couple of years.

This pervasive sense of regret and sheer emotional rawness of the song is reminiscent of Mat Johnson circa *Soul Mining*.

'Nine years ago I fell in love, with a lady proud and fair / so passionate were she and I we made fire in the air'... 'I was brutal, I was ignorant, I was cruel, I was brash / I never gave a damn about the beauty that I'd smashed / No sadist I yet found delight in making my love cry / now I pray for a single kiss from her, to be lashed and crucified.'

If there were any doubts about whether MacGowan still had the talent of his youth, here was ample proof positive that he was not completely washed up. Using an old traditional arrangement, it comes as a surprise after hearing all the reports of an increasingly bitter MacGowan who had locked himself away in a studio to write songs that were going to be more like lyrical punch-ups with the people he felt had let him down over the last few years.

One of those people was supposed to be Van Morrison, who has been a friend of MacGowan and his girlfriend Victoria Clarke for some time. MacGowan included *Victoria* on the album, a song written for her which includes the lines, 'Victoria, left me in opium euphoria / with a fat monk singing Gloria'. This is not the first time that MacGowan has made reference to Morrison as a rival in the love stakes. When both performed at the Finsbury Fleadh in 1983, MacGowan discovered Morrison in 'an amorous clinch with a lady friend', and legend has it, promptly quipped, 'from now it is Van The Other Man'.

It is difficult to know how serious the whole thing is, for while there is no doubt that there has been friction between the two characters, they often appear together both socially and on-stage. In typical MacGowan fashion he states that the 'fat monk' in question is one he met while in the Far East on holiday a few years ago.

During a series of carefully selected appearances in the run up to the release of the album, MacGowan joined Christy Moore on *The Late Late Show* for a rousing version of *Spancil Hill*. He looked well, and the duet went well, but when he took off his sunglasses it seemed as if he had suddenly aged ten years. His eyes which could switch from manic glaring to doe-like innocence in one blink were dulled and, while not exactly lifeless, they reminded you of just how much he has gone through in the past few years.

It would be pointless to wonder if these years have made him a stronger person given that the priority throughout the late 1980s and after was simply survival, but while there is no doubt that *The Snake* is a flawed work, it is a hell of a lot better than anybody had really expected.

The aforementioned *The Song With No Name*, the strange but brilliant *Her Father Never Liked Me Anyway* and *Victoria*, all good songs are probably worth the price of buying the album, but there is no doubt that he has a long way to climb before he can reach the sublime heights of his earlier works with The Pogues.

Of course, there are a lot of people who don't think he will ever reclaim his talent to that extent, and they may be right. But MacGowan is a man who has been dying of the same hangover for the last ten years and it hasn't put him under yet.

Whatever happens to MacGowan over the next few years (and that could be anything from total artistic rejuvenation to an early grave) we can count on at least one thing, it will be, like him, a fascinating spectacle.

DISCOGRAPHY

SINGLES WITH THE NIPPLE ERECTORS/ THE NIPS

King Of The Bop / Nervous Wreck
All The Time In The World / All The Time In The World
Gabrielle
Happy Song / Nobody To Love
Rocks Off Records (1976 / 1977)

SINGLES WITH THE POGUES

Dark Streets Of London / The Band Played Waltzing Matilda
Pogue Mahone Records PM1 (May 1984)

Dark Streets Of London / The Band Played Waltzing Matilda
Stiff Records BUY 207 (June 1984)

Boys From The County Hell / Repeal Of The Licensing Laws
Stiff Records BUY 212 (October 1984)

A Pair Of Brown Eyes / Whiskey You're The Devil
Stiff Records BUY 220 (March 1985)

A Pair Of Brown Eyes / Whiskey You're The Devil / Muirchin Dirkin
Stiff Records 12" BUYIT 220 (March 1985)

Sally MacLennane / Wild Rover
Stiff Records BUY 224 (June 1985)

Sally MacLennane / Wild Rover / The Leaving Of Liverpool
Stiff Records 12" BUYIT 224 (June 1985)

Dirty Old Town / A Pistol For Paddy Garcia
Stiff Records BUY 229 (August 1985)

Dirty Old Town / A Pistol For Paddy Garcia / The Parting Glass
Stiff Records 12" BUYIT 229 (August 1985)

Haunted / Junk Theme
MCA Records 1084 (August 1986) *

Haunted / Junk Theme / Hot Dogs With Everything
MCA Records 12" MCAT 1084 (August 1986)

The Irish Rover / The Rare Ould Mountain Dew
Stiff Records BUY 258 (March 1987) (With The Dubliners)

The Irish Rover / The Rare Ould Mountain Dew / The Dubliners
Fancy
Stiff Records 12" BUYIT 258 (March 1987) (With The Dubliners)

Fairytale Of New York / Battle March Medley
Pogue Mahone NY 7 (November 1987) (With Kirsty MacColl)

---

*From the LP 'Sid & Nancy – Love Kills' MCA MCG 6011
(July 1986)

Fairytale Of New York / Battle March Medley / Shanne Bradley
Pogue Mahone 12" NY 12 (November 1987) (With Kirsty MacColl)

If I Should Fall From Grace With God / Sally MacLennane (live)
Pogue Mahone FG1 (February 1988)

If I Should Fall From Grace With God / Sally MacLennane (live) /
A Pair Of Brown Eyes (live)
Pogue Mahone 12" FG 112 (February 1988)

Fiesta / Sketches Of Spain
Pogue Mahone FG 2 (July 1988)

Fiesta / Sketches Of Spain / South Australia
Pogue Mahone 12" FG 212 (July 1988)

WITH NICK CAVE
What A Wonderful World
Mute Records (November 1992)

WITH THE POPES
The Church Of The Holy Spook / That Woman's Got Me Drinking

ALBUMS (With The Pogues)
RED ROSES FOR ME

Transmetropolitan / The Battle Of Brisbane / The Auld Triangle /
Waxies Dargle / Boys From The County Hell / Sea Shanty / Dark
Streets Of London / Streams Of Whiskey / Poor Paddy / Dingle

Regatta / Greenland Whale Fisheries / Down In The Ground Where The Dead Men Go / Kitty

Stiff Records SEEZ 55 (October 1984)

RUM, SODOMY AND THE LASH

The Sick Bed Of Cuchulainn / The Old Main Drag / Wild Cats Of Kilkenny / A Pair Of Brown Eyes / I'm A Man You Don't Meet Every Day / Dirty Old Town / Jesse James / Billy's Bones / Navigator / The Gentleman Soldier / And The Band Played Waltzing Matilda / A Pistol For Paddy Garcia **

Stiff Records SEEZ 58 (August 1985)

**Included on cassette and CD only

STRAIGHT TO HELL : THE ORIGINAL SOUNDTRACK

The Good, The Bad And The Ugly / Rake At The Gates Of Hell / If I Should Fall From Grace With God / Rabinga / Danny Boy

Stiff Records DIABLO 1 (July 1987)

IF I SHOULD FALL FROM GRACE WITH GOD

If I Should Fall From Grace With God / Turkish Song Of The Damned / Bottle Of Smoke / Fairytale Of New York / Metropolis / Thousands Are Sailing / Fiesta / Medley - Recruiting Sergeant, Rocky Road To Dublin, Galway Races / Streets Of Sorrow / Birmingham Six / Lullaby Of London / Sit Down By The Fire / The Broad Majestic Shannon / Worms / South Australia* / The Battle March Medley**

Pogue Mahone NYR 1 (January 1988)

*/** Only available on cassette and CD versions

PEACE AND LOVE
Gridlock / White City / Young Ned Of The Hill / Misty Morning
Albert Bridge / Cotton Fields / Blue Heaven / Down All The
Days / USA / Lorelei / Gartloney Rats / Boat Train / Tombstone /
Night Train To Lorca / London You're A Lady
Warner Bros. 1989

HELLS DITCH
Sunnyside Of The Street / Sayonara / Ghost Of A Smile / Hells
Ditch / Lorcas Novena / Summer In Siam / Rain Street /
Rainbow Man / Wake Of The Medusa / House Of The Gods / 5
Green Queens And Jean / Maidrin Rua / Six To Go
Warner Bros. 1991

WITH THE POPES
THE SNAKE
The Church Of The Holy Spook / That Woman's Got Me Drinking /
The Song With No Name / Aisling / I'll Be Your Hand Bag / Her
Father Didn't Like Me Anyway / A Mexican Funeral In Paris / The
Snake With Eyes Of Garnet / Donegal Express / Victoria / The
Rising Of The Moon / Bring Down The Lamp
Warner Bros. Records (October 1994)